MAY'S BARN
DANCING

BEAVER FEED CO.
ULTRA-LIFED
for POULTRY-DOGS and all LIVING CREATURES.

BILL'S
A&W
DRIVE-IN
TROY, MICHIGAN

One Cup at a Time

Why a Gaggle of Geezers Gathers
Every Monday Morning
To Solve the World's Problems

For: Dan Palin

Thanks for all you do

Dennis Ritter

Chap 6

One Cup at a Time

Why a Gaggle of Geezers Gathers
Every Monday Morning
To Solve the World's Problems

A MEMOIR

Edited by Bill Haney

First published in the United States
by MB Books

MB Books, a unit of MB Communications, LLC
2820 Hummer Lake Road
Ortonville, MI 48462

For information about this and other books by the editor,
visit billhaneybooks.com

Ordering information about this book may be found in the back of this book.

ISBN 978-0-9845651-1-5

Cover, montages, and text design by Jacinta Calcut
Image Graphics & Design
image-gd.com

Photograph of authors in the back of this book by Meghan Graney

Printed in the United States of America
by Edwards Brothers Malloy
Ann Arbor, Michigan

Lives of great men all remind us
  We can make our lives sublime,
And, departing, leave behind us
  Footprints on the sands of time

"A Psalm of Life"
Henry Wadsworth Longfellow

For those who walked the journeys alongside us
and left their own footprints in the sands of time

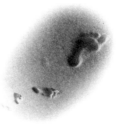

CONTENTS

FOREWORD

THERE WERE SO many memorable moments for me personally during my eight years as Michigan's governor. But none were more gratifying than those totally unexpected yet priceless moments when someone I never met before came up to tell me their own personal story.

What they said may have had absolutely nothing to do with the business of the state. It might have concerned a problem they alone were dealing with, hoping I could somehow do something about it. That wasn't always possible. Too often all I could do was respond with words of understanding, to listen, and to care. It was easy to tell when a person simply wanted to see if there was anyone in government who gave a hoot about what was going on in the lives of regular citizens. Sometimes, the person was bursting with passion for a cause they were involved in and wanted to tell me why they were so committed to that cause. As they talked, they were also telling me about something fundamental about who they were as a person.

Whatever the motivation or the subject, these personal stories stuck with me. They are indelible memories of my eight years as governor of a state that is second to none in the contributions its citizens have made to this nation.

Not every person feels comfortable approaching an elected official and that, by the way, is a sad commentary on how distant many people in government become from the people they are supposed to be representing. So I know that for each one of those stories, there were a hundred, a thousand, or more that I never got to hear. So many stories that never got told.

That's one of the reasons I was delighted to write this foreword for a book that captures so poignantly the real-life stories of eleven Michiganders. One of the many charms of this book is that these are not accounts of one stunning accomplishment after another by a well-known business leader, entertainment figure, or sports star. Michigan does have many movers and shakers and books have been written by or about many of them. On the contrary, it's likely that you never heard of most of the people you will read about in the following pages, even though, as you will see, they are intriguing in their own right and have quietly made meaningful contributions.

Their stories are representative of the many productive, community-minded folks we have in this wonderful state of Michigan. That should come as no surprise when you think about what our people—especially our seniors—have been through. All of these eleven authors endured the depths or the aftermath of the Great Depression, World War II, the chilling Cold War, and far too many military actions and health scares. But so did the citizens of every other state in the Union.

What was different in Michigan is that because of the nature of its economy over the decades, our families took economic body blows sooner, and the pain was deeper, more pervasive, and lingered longer. They had to withstand so many other severe shocks peculiar to this state, including the smoldering strife between large corporate managements and labor that burst into flames with the Flint GM sit-down strike that gave national clout, thankfully, to the United Auto Workers.

Every downturn in the national economy hit the Detroit Big Three the hardest, throwing thousands out of work, sometimes for extended periods. Virtually every job in the state depended in some way on a healthy automobile industry. That meant that any slowdown in that business sector cast a pall over the entire state. And that is why my vision for Michigan was an economy with healthy diversification teamed with a strong automotive-based sector, a healthy balance to avoid those steep declines that throw workers out of jobs.

The people who told their stories in *One Cup at a Time* somehow made it through those trying times. How did they do it? How did they go on to make a living, make a career, and even make their mark in so many fields? The stories of how they prevailed and brought up their own children into better conditions than they themselves enjoyed are stories worth reading. Here are real-life examples of the resiliency of the human spirit.

Another striking feature of this book is the similarity of experiences these people went through, and yet how dissimilar were the outcomes. Nearly all of them had not one career or two, but often several, and some had lots. Their chosen fields ran a dizzying gamut, but they followed a pattern that is typical of the zigs and zags taken by most Michigan senior citizens—that is, adversity triggered diversity. Put another way, they all shared the conviction that when it comes to caring for your family, there is no such thing as a bad job.

Born in the Dust Bowl of Nebraska in the depths of the Great Depression, Gerald McNally moved with his family to Detroit where he spent his teenage years. He did his military service in Greenland and then was a crewman on Great Lakes ore carriers. A voracious reader and visionary student of philosophy, he could not have foreseen that his U-M law degree and a series of chance events would elevate him to the bench as a District Court judge for thirty-four years, that the first assisted suicide case involving Jack Kevorkian would come before him.

Carole Cotter Bodner grew up in the pre-Troy village of Big Beaver where she first learned coping skills, perseverance, and a steely work ethic. She would later draw on those resources to crack through the gender walls in military and technology fields and go on to excel in role after role as she implemented sophisticated system software conversions on government projects from the Chesapeake Bay to San Diego.

Wally Niezguski bounced from managing Detroit's Playboy Club to running a ski resort to fishing commercially for salmon. In just a few of his many untraditional jobs, he processed medical X-rays and chemicals to glean their silver content, owned a ranch, served as a marshal in the West, and owned a bakery. Finally he segued into the cultivation of pure organic vegetables and free-range chicken eggs that people drive miles to buy at his small Independence Township farm, donating some of his bounty to feed the needy.

A remarkable feature of these stories is how good-natured, even humorous and poignant, they are. You might think that someone who had been through so many dark and troubling days in childhood and teenage years would grow up to be a dispirited adult, would finally throw up their hands and say, "Why me, Lord, why me?" But no. Again and again the attitude we read about here springs from a deep well—draws from the same strength of character I saw in Michigan men and women while I served as their Attorney General and Governor: "Okay, life has knocked me down. But self-pity is for wimps. Could have been worse, so get back up and get on with it."

Invariably, for Michigan women and men in those years in the mid-Twentieth Century, getting on with it meant adapting, even if that meant changing careers.

For Dennis Ritter it meant going from high school in Pontiac to an Army uniform in Vietnam and the violent wakeup call from the Viet Cong known as the Tet Offensive. Then, thanks to the GI Bill, to an economics degree from the University of Michigan, he traced a circuitous route to become a township trustee, treasurer and supervisor, as well as a farm market owner, and Clarkston city manager.

Dale Bond' s childhood years saw him moving between Depression-days Detroit and his grandparents' farm in western Michigan. From there it was on to the typical succession of jobs in Detroit car factories, only to be interrupted by a hitch in the Air Force. Then, after fifteen years designing dies for manufacturers, he began to exploit his talents as an inventor. He took out twenty-four patents as he built highly efficient industrial systems for the automotive industry in a company he founded where he created hundreds of new jobs.

And the list goes on. Mel Vaara went from a small mining community in the Upper Peninsula to an invigorating college experience and a fine education at Northern Michigan University. That gave him the foundation for his long, outstanding career in leadership roles in school administration in Clarkston and in other settings. Another "Yooper" who migrated to north Oakland County after traveling widely is Buck Kopietz. From early days in Manistique, Buck served in the Coast Guard before finishing his degree at Oakland University, then ultimately opening the doors of Millpond B & B, bringing visitors to Clarkston from all over the world. Downstate, Jim Reed grew up in Flint when it was called a GM factory town, and went on to a long career there before shifting his own gears to the preservation of our pristine natural areas.

Each story in these chapters is a chronicle of rebounding from a setback, seizing opportunity, showing the kind of resourcefulness and staying power that have fueled so many comebacks in Michigan. It's as if people could handle anything after living uneasily for decades with total dependence upon a single-industry economy. They could even reinvent themselves while facing up to the possible extinction of the entire Michigan automobile industry and the specter of economic catastrophe.

Confronting reality is precisely what these people did.

Confronting it, then dealing with it. Year after year. Then, after five or so decades in jobs or occupations, long after they might have eased gently into their golden years, they are still active and productive. They continue to devote their time, energies and resources to the betterment of their communities, to teach and to learn, to reach out a hand to help a neighbor or a stranger.

Bob McGowan, a marketing executive and a thespian, is a typical example. Twenty-five years ago, he founded Bittersweet Farm Plant-A-Row Community Garden. There, master gardeners and volunteers like his Monday morning coffee compatriot Carole Cotter Bodner, tend land that in a bountiful year yields as much as two-and-a-half tons of nutritious organic vegetables. All that produce goes to help feed the needy in nearby distressed communities.

Many people in this book worked in a succession of very different realms. After careers in the aerospace and marketing industries, Bill Haney returned to his more literary roots and published many essays, articles and books about Michigan. As if that weren't enough, he reinvigorated major book-publishing entities, including the University of Michigan Press. Then he founded his own companies to produce an array of definitive books on Michigan themes, and launched Ernie Harwell's post-broadcast career as an author, among many others.

Anyone seeking inspiring stories of the strength and durability of the human spirit need look no further than the pages of this book for convincing proof that you don't have to be a prominent public figure to make a difference. Not only that, these personal accounts make for reading that is both enjoyable and inspiring.

Although this was the first time I heard these particular stories, none of this really surprises me. Not for a second, because I would have expected no less from a group of progressive-thinking Michiganders who meet every Monday morning in Clarkston for one cup of coffee at a time while they solve the world's problems—even though they know they'll just have to come right back to Brioni Cafe again next Monday morning to do it all over again.

Former Governor Jennifer Granholm
October 19, 2016

PREFACE

IN READING THESE pages, the thought may flicker from time to time that there are recurring themes here. That is because much of what was happening with the eleven authors of these chapters during those long-ago decades was unexceptional. Millions of families in every one of the forty-eight states were enduring the same miseries and deprivations. Fathers without jobs, mothers worried sick over undernourished kids, they sat night after night at the kitchen table, brooding over the same worries. Yet, through it all, appreciating the good, of which there was certainly some, and most of all, simply enduring and, at last, prevailing.

Prevailing. That is at the heart of this book. It is, indeed, the reason each of these authors opened doors closed long ago, to dig deep into the recesses of memory, to resurrect and write down what happened. The good times and the not-so-good. It was seldom easy; it was sometimes painful to revisit those bygone days and to see now with sharper clarity and a fresh perspective how the travails of their youth shaped the adult they became. So, they told their story, lest it be lost forever to their descendants and to posterity.

We see that there was life in Oakland County, in Michigan, in this country long before television. Before computers. Before dependable cars and Saran Wrap. There was radio and there were comic books and *The Saturday Evening Post* and Saturday matinees with double features for a dime. But central heating and air conditioning existed only in science fiction. There was—usually, but not always—food that you actually grew or raised yourself, long before Big Macs at the drive-through and pizza delivered to the door.

That will come as no news flash to most of the readers of

this book who will, themselves, have lived through the same succession of The Great Depression, the Second World War, the specter of polio, the Cold War, a few more recessions, influenza epidemics, and several military interventions. But these stories of the way it was in America then, will, perhaps, via the magic of the eBook edition of this volume, shed some light into dark corners of younger minds. Little doubt that the adolescents of today will, in turn, one day reflect back onto their own childhood and formative years. They may then reminisce about their own old times, say in the year 2016, when, if you can imagine it, there were actually automobiles that weren't really "auto" at all but to get anywhere you had to steer and manipulate pedals and levers instead of just saying to some disembodied computer entity, "Drive to Oakland County Farmers Market... and don't spare the horses."

Those future years may be chock-full of wonders and the joys of living on a planet that has finally been treated kindly by its human inhabitants, that is no longer teeming with wretched starving souls mired in poverty and disease.

Would that this bucolic future prove prophetic, this dream of a clean and tranquil world. More's the pity, the history of mankind since fire and the wheel were discovered does not inspire optimism. But, could happen. If it does, and if people still read books and still care about the ideas in those books and are curious about the people who wrote them, then this is our bequest. To those future generations— our own descendants and anyone with the itch of curiosity— these stories will have to stand as our humble testaments.

This is how it was for eleven of those who came before you, in and around Clarkston, in Oakland and neighboring counties. Some never left. Others traveled to every state in the Union and untold miles around the world only to return, drawn back by whatever force, to have coffee every Monday morning at Brioni's Cafe & Deli, Clarkston, Michigan, to solve yet again and until next week, the problems of the world.

INTRODUCTION

THIS BOOK IS evidence that it is not only the "great men" of whom Longfellow wrote who can leave "footprints on the sands of time."

Everyone you will encounter in these pages had humble beginnings. As Dale Bond, an astute observer of the human condition and author of a chapter herein, has noted, "You can pull yourself up by your bootstraps, but your feet still remain on the ground."

In their childhood days and younger years, it was plenty enough for these eleven authors to just get a pair of boots to wear, and then with years of hard work and persistence, perhaps to get a bit ahead. Not much time spent in idle dreaming about getting rich or famous.

Yet, in a more fundamental and lasting sense, these are also stories of success. That is, if you define success as someone managing to make the absolute best of the hand they were dealt. Each exploited fully his or her genetic endowment, made the most of the limited resources in their immediate environment, and was ever alert to unexpected opportunities. They prevailed against considerable odds to succeed in not only one field of endeavor, but frequently in two or three or more careers.

Some of those later years are touched on by a few of these writers but by others not at all. That's because one note that rings throughout this book is what was going on locally, in Michigan, and in the greater world during those formative years. These were lives forged in the crucibles of the 1930s through the 1950s.

As Jennifer Granholm has recounted in her Foreword, those were tumultuous and trying times. The Great Depression. The Dust Bowl. The looming storms of fascism and empire-building just over the horizon, across the Atlantic and the Pacific. The comparative safety and comfort of America exploded with World War II, its carnage and its aftermaths, including the specter of nuclear conflict. These were powerful forces buffeting everyone's life.

In some ways, the stories are quite similar, one to another. In even more ways, they are completely unique. Being a youngster in those years often meant accepting deprivation as the norm. For some, it meant enduring a barrage of blows that would crush the spirit of many people of today used to such "luxuries" as food, heat, and shelter. But as William Faulkner insisted in his 1950 Nobel Prize acceptance speech:

> *I believe that man will not merely endure: he will prevail. He is immortal, not because he alone among creatures has an inexhaustible voice, but because he has a soul, a spirit capable of compassion and sacrifice and endurance. The poet's, the writer's, duty is to write about these things. It is his privilege to help man endure by lifting his heart, by reminding him of the courage and honor and hope and pride and compassion and pity and sacrifice which have been the glory of his past.*

If everyone alive in America in those days was impacted by these forces, it is fair to ask, What is exceptional about the people in this book?

The answer is, probably not much, and, at the same time, a lot.

In many ways, the dozen or so people in these chapters are extraordinarily ordinary. That fact in itself carries a lesson. Each of us is the sum of the many forces that have impinged on us: the genes we inherited and over which we have not the slightest control; the environment in which we grew from infancy in those delicate, formative years; the experiences we incorporated into ourselves and how we dealt with them; and the people we encountered all along the way and how they shaped us and how we perhaps shaped them.

As Mark Twain wrote of so powerfully in his unfinished novel, *The Mysterious Stranger*, one seemingly trivial act, simply turning left instead of right at an intersection and bumping into a stranger can change a life, and perhaps many lives, profoundly. The lives written about in these pages are no exception. A chance meeting, a decision made on a whim— a new future unfolds.

How I happened to come into the group is a case in point.

One day, curious about a sign I had passed several times on Sashabaw Road proclaiming "Wally's Organic Veggies," I pulled over to have a look. I had my own small garden, but had been reading articles about vegetables, especially some pieces published by my daughter Jessica, a very savvy and cautious mother. She writes of how essential it is to good health to eat totally organic and preferably locally grown produce. Talking with proprietor Wally Niezguski as I admired his black krim tomatoes and Polish garlic bulbs, it was obvious he raised not only good food for the body, but also served up intriguing food for thought. The bottom line is pretty much: "Don't eat a vegetable you don't know personally."

Wally invited me to have coffee some Monday morning with eight to ten friends at a restaurant in nearby Clarkston. My glib reply was something like, "Thanks, but I don't need any new friends. Actually, I'm trying to get rid of some of the old ones." Wally laughed politely, and persisted. For about three years.

In the meantime, whenever I stopped at his veggie stand,

we talked enough about social issues that I could see we were bent similarly toward the progressive pole of the political globe. Still, I turn and run rapidly away from people I even agree with if all they do is parrot yet another egomaniacal cable channel pundit. Wally finally wore me down. He assured me that the folks he shared coffee with were a diverse group, yes, but they had in common an unapologetically open, socially conscious, and liberal slant on the world.

It took only a couple cups of fresh-brewed coffee along with a lemon poppyseed muffin one Monday morning at Brioni Cafe & Deli to confirm that Wally was right. He had cultivated as sharply focused an appreciation of the attitudes and demeanors of these people as he did meticulously for his heirloom tomatoes.

What began as a one-time visit to mollify Wally soon became an inked-in time of the week. I mentioned this to my son Mark and after a few weeks he made a suggestion so obvious it somehow had never occurred to me, even though in the previous fifty years I had had a hand in creating several hundred books in one way or another. Get each of them to write a chapter, Mark suggested, mostly about how it was growing up in the 1940s and '50s. Nearly all of them had spent their childhood in southeastern Michigan, all but a few in the cities, towns, or farmland north of Detroit.

One of the first questions the group had to consider was whether it would be worth the time and energy it would take to exhume those stories from the dusty chambers of long-ago decades. I explained that was the question any publisher had to ask about a prospective book before going one step further. I told them I had heard that same question in May 1984 over a cup of coffee in the broadcast booth at Briggs Stadium. I had just urged the long-time Detroit Tigers play-by-play announcer to get his own story down for posterity. "Aw, hard to believe anybody would be interested in my little stories, twenty-second snippets between pitches," he said.

Turned out there were plenty of stories for Ernie Harwell to eventually write half a dozen books that provided him a fulfilling post-broadcast career. Ernie's first book, *Tuned to Baseball*, sold in the tens of thousands of copies, a best-seller.

Toting up copies sold and profits made, however, is only one way to measure the success of a book, and, to my mind, not the best one. There are many other ways, one of which is as simple as the warm and fuzzy feeling it was worth cutting down a tree to get the pulp to make the book. For *One Cup at a Time*, it was a given that the primary audience for this book would be small. Most interested readers would be found in the communities in which the authors have lived and worked, along with people who liked to read personal accounts of what life was like in the middle of the turbulent Twentieth Century. All the authors agreed that the venture was a success if even one reader gleaned an insight, was touched in a meaningful way by one of these chapters.

As the project began to take shape, a personal portrait began to emerge of what life was like in those days spanning the Great Depression, World War II, the Cold War, and the Fifties. These were written as personal experiences, but at the same time, these stories reflected what went on in the lives of virtually everyone in America in those days.

Several of the authors had initially doubted they could retrieve much from those long-ago days. Or were skeptical that those recollections would be of much interest to anyone else. Some of the writers said that for years they had avoided reflecting on those early years because growing up hungry and sometimes without even the barest necessities was not a particularly enjoyable memory.

However, once they were into the process, they discovered

that the memories were there all along, even if sometimes indistinct or totally blocked out beyond the folds in the curtain of time. Then, as they tugged at one thread, the curtain obscuring the past began to unravel. They kept at it until eventually they could see clearly what had lain hidden and unconsidered for years, for most of a lifetime ago. They also discovered something surprising: there were a lot of good times, too, and experiences that they now could see were important in shaping them into the person they became.

As the process went forward, each contributor read the chapters of each fellow author. They found, in each chapter, some eye-openers, even sometimes a *Wow!* factor. Here were eleven people who thought there wasn't much to learn about the people they had been sitting with at Brioni's round table for several years. They were wrong, of course.

They were wrong because it would be hard for anyone who has been around for seven, even eight decades, *not* to have some good stories to tell. The roadblock that few are able to get past is knowing how best to tell those stories and, once getting the story written, how to get the stories in front of people who might be interested in reading them.

⌒

WELL, THE PEOPLE in this book did it. They knew you don't have to be someone who has done things that have changed the world. Precious few have done that. It's sufficient for a well-lived life that a person has made something of a mark on the lives of others. And that is something that the people in the following pages have done. How they did it. Why they did it. These are more than simple stories—they serve as lessons for us all and are now preserved as their footprints in the sands of time.

Bill Haney
October 19, 2016

1

FARMS, FAMILY, FACTORIES, & FRIENDS
by Dale Bond

*"I watched in awe as a long line of mounted troops
rode past the farm. Near the end of the line, horses
pulled heavy artillery pieces. It was the grandest
parade I have ever seen."*

In 1928, MY father, Noel, left the family farm in Salem Township, Allegan County. That was the year he married Jenny Freeman, his high school sweetheart, and moved to Detroit where he found work as a letter carrier. I was born in April 1929 in a house on Robinwood Street. We later moved to Pilgrim Street in northwest Detroit where, except for periods living in the country with relatives, I lived until my graduation from Cooley High School in June 1947.

After the 1929 stock market crash, the country sank into the depths of the Great Depression. As a young boy I did not know what that meant to our family. My sister Virginia was born in July 1931 in Harper Hospital. In our small two-bedroom house on Pilgrim Street, I slept in the same bed as my sister, until I was about seven or eight years old, something that was not unusual and certainly not alarming in those days. As children we thought our lives were normal. A usual meal would be rice and raisins, milk toast, vegetables, and, on rare occasions, liver.

Dad could not afford to buy a house so we were renters, as were most others on our block. I remember a Mr. Harris, a large man with red hair. He would visit every month with a thick book listing the houses on which he would collect the monthly rent—always in cash. Rent was thirty dollars a month. Although Dad didn't make much money, we kids didn't think of ourselves as poor because we had food and clothes. Not only that, Dad had a car while many neighbors did not.

The house was heated with a big furnace in the basement into which Dad shoveled coal with a scoop shovel. The hot water tank was galvanized steel and not insulated, and so I would light the natural gas burner with a match an hour or so before I could take a bath. Then I would make a trip down to the basement and put my hand on the tank to feel whether the water would be hot.

The ice box was cooled by a block of ice with a drip tray underneath. We put large cardboard signs in the front windows so the men delivering ice, coal, and milk would see what to deliver. Every house had a milk chute where the milkman would leave full bottles of milk and blocks of butter and pick up empty bottles. The milk chute had inside and outside doors just big enough for a small child to squeeze through when someone had left the house key inside and the door was locked. A few times it was necessary for me to perform that task.

Milk and ice were delivered by horse-drawn wagons. The milk was not homogenized and there was about three inches of cream on top—Mother would pour off some for coffee before shaking the bottle. The back of the ice wagon was open and there were always chips of ice to be found there. We kids were always delighted to find a mouth-size ice chip and would suck on it as content as if it were a piece of store-bought candy. The delivery horses would often leave souvenirs on the pavement. A neighbor would go out with a shovel to retrieve those gifts for his flower garden.

Because the garages were behind the houses with an alley for access, house lots were narrow without room for side driveways. We saved newspapers, tied them with twine, and sold them to the man who went through the alleys with a horse and wagon and a hand-held scale so he could buy papers and scrap metal by weight. We called him "the Sheeny man," a nickname we heard and used without knowing what, if anything, it meant. Today they would call such a fellow a scrapper.

We kids used the alley more than we did the front sidewalks. We were all "pickers," and there were good things to find. One day while looking for stuff, I picked up a bottle of pills. Thinking they must be good since they made people feel better. I put a pill in my mouth. Yuck! I spit it out. Lesson learned.

One day I found something I would never forget. In a paper bag in a trash can, I found a dead baby. It caused quite a commotion and the neighbors congregated in the alley and talked among themselves about it. It got lots of attention in the neighborhood but I never heard the slightest thing about how such a thing could happen.

The younger boys often learned something new from the older kids. One older boy tried to introduce us younger boys to smoking. He peeled the paper off a cigarette butt, put the tobacco in a pipe, lit it and gave it to a young friend who in turn passed it to me for a puff. Instead of inhaling, I blew everything out of the pipe. That was the first and last time I ever put tobacco in my mouth.

I remember a World War I veteran without legs. We would see him come slowly down our street. He positioned himself on a low platform with wheels and propelled himself with his arms and hands. He had a megaphone and sang old favorites. There was a tin cup mounted on his platform for donations. People would yell out tunes for him to sing. I still remember one of his songs, *Springtime in the Rockies*. Some of the neighbor men on our street would flip coins from their porches to boys who would deposit them in the tin cup.

Some years earlier, in 1935, when I was six years old, tragedy had struck my family. My mother became ill. My father took my sister and me to live with relatives back in Allegan. My sister stayed on a farm with Aunt Grace, my mother's sister. I stayed in the town of Allegan with my dad's sister, Beryl; it was there that I started school and lived until 1937.

One day that year when I was at grandmother's house on her farm, we got a phone call that changed our lives. The old crank phone was on a five-party line that rang in all the households nearby. There were five different rings—such as two short, one long—combinations that everyone on the line knew. So everyone was aware who was getting a call. On that day, the phone rang again and again for a very long time. I had to ask grandmother to answer it. She said it wasn't her call, but after a while, since it kept ringing, she picked it up. It was Central—the operator—calling to advise grandmother that my mother had died. It was only later that I learned that my father also had lost his mother, in 1914, when he was seven years old, so he too had grown up without the mother who gave birth to him.

Days later, the large front yard of grandmother's house was full of automobiles of neighbors and friends who had come for the funeral service. The casket was in the corner of the parlor and folding chairs had been brought in for the mourners. My sister Virginia remembers that Uncle Bob lifted her up so she could see mother in the tall white casket. Thinking back on Mother's last days, Virginia remembers that just days before the doctor had made a house call. Virginia was sent outside while the doctor was attending to Mother for what must have been one final time.

I have one memory—and one memory only—of my mother. I remember a spanking she gave me and my sister, Virginia, one summer day. It was hot and so the windows were open. We both screamed and howled so loudly and so long that Mr. Dodeman, our next-door neighbor came over to see what was the cause of the commotion. We were bawling not from the pain of the spanking but just because we were angry that we were getting a spanking for any reason. What we understood only later was that our mother was very ill.

Soon we were sent to grandmother's house on the farm. It was not because my sister and I were naughty but because the stress of two energetic youngsters was simply more than my mother could bear, so that is why Dad had to take us away. That was the last time that I saw my mother alive.

I have many fond memories of the time I spent at Gramma and Grampa Freeman's farm. Gramma and Grampa spoke Dutch. If my mother had not died, I believe that today I would also know that language. Gramma had a heart of gold. Her table was often laden with "raising bread," mounds of dough rising from yeast and covered with towels. The aroma of her bread baking in the oven is as unforgettable as it was delicious.

Gramma had false teeth that didn't fit very well and made a clicking sound I can hear to this day. Grampa was a quiet man. He had a favorite place to sit in a corner behind a wood-burning stove where it was warm and cozy. He chewed tobacco which stained his teeth. When he wanted Gramma, whose name was Fannie, he would yell, "Fen-nah!"

The telephone, which was mounted on the wall in the kitchen was a wooden box with two large bells. That was the phone that rang over and over on that fateful day that changed lives for our family.

During a rain storm, you got away from that phone because when lightning struck nearby, a flare of electricity might come flashing out of the phone. Eventually the wall phones and the party lines gave way to new technology and equipment. The wall phones were obsoleted by smaller phones that sat on a table or a desk. The phone company didn't bother to collect the wall phones and so the farmers, being thrifty as well as handy with such things, found a way to use them. They rigged up their own system using these old phones, keeping the connections with other homes with which they had shared the party lines. So they ended up with not only the new phones with private lines, but also they now had their own separate phone system using the old wall phones.

~

MY DAD RETURNED to Detroit while my sister and I remained with Aunt Grace and Uncle Harm. They did not have children and wanted to adopt us. Dad remarried. His new wife had been his housekeeper and she became my step-mother. Dad came to Allegan and took us back to Detroit. I heard that he was criticized for his quick marriage. I was told later by Uncle Bob, my mother's brother, that there had been intense pressure from Aunt Grace for him to take over raising my sister and me and that was what prompted Dad's re-marriage.

~

FOR THE NEXT few years, every summer vacation from school, Dad took us to the farm of Aunt Grace and Uncle Harm and there we would stay until the new school semester. Dad's mother had died when he was seven, and so he had grown up without a mother. I am sure he did not want the same fate to befall my sister and me.

Those summers were great. I loved farming and it didn't bother me that the house had no electricity or running water. The outhouse, as was typical, was located some fifty feet away. Also, as was usual, the amenities included the customary Sears catalog (intended for reading, of course).

Aunt Grace and Uncle Harm never missed church service or worked on Sunday, except for the necessary chores of milking and feeding animals and chickens. The church held two services, with the early one in Dutch and the second one in English. Because sister Virginia and I did not know Dutch, we went to the English service.

It was many years before there would be air conditioning and the church was stifling hot. Hand fans were provided—stashed alongside hymn books in the compartments on the backs of pew—and that was very necessary. It was a great relief when the service ended and we could go outside where people gathered and talked with neighbors. Often that was the opportunity for people to extend an invitation a visit on Sunday evening, after chore time when there would be time for quiet conversations The women chatted in Dutch amongst themselves while the men talked and smoked their pipes.

After a couple hours, Aunt Grace would say "coffee-hem," and then serve coffee and cookies. That was the signal that the visit would soon end, a polite way to tell guests it was time to go. I can vividly recall those happy times and traditions that are sorely missed.

Meals were an important part of life on the farm. Before every meal, Uncle Harm would ask for a minute of silent grace. We sat with our heads bowed until Uncle Harm would make a loud sniff through his nose, his signal that finally we could eat. Some rituals and behaviors were especially significant for him and he expected us to observe them. When the dish of breads and buns was passed to me, I might touch one and then change my mind and reach for a different one. "Don't finger the food," Uncle Harm would say with a stern look at me. Throughout the meal, I could feel his eyes, sharp as a hawk's, making sure I was minding my manners.

Most of the meat came from animals raised on the farm, but because of all the other work they had to do, Uncle Harm and Aunt Grace didn't do much gardening. So they bought most of the vegetables from the local grocery store. The grocer closed the store one day a week and delivered right to the house. He had a truck he had rigged up where you could walk in from the back and there were shelves along the side with canned goods and he would bring all kinds of canned goods to the house.

Some of the locals were handy that same way, taking old Model T automobiles and making modifications to turn them into small tractors for utility work around the farm.

⌁

THE SUMMER OF 1938 at Uncle Harm's farm was an especially exciting time for me, a nine-year-old boy. The Army was having War Games. There were two large groups of soldiers wearing World War I uniforms with large-brimmed hats. One group had a red band on the hat, the others a blue band. They were cavalry and all were on horseback.

I watched in awe as a long line of mounted troops rode past the farm. Near the end of the line, horses pulled heavy artillery pieces. It was the grandest parade I have ever seen.

The country roads were not gravel but instead were two ruts about six inches deep that had been carved into the grass fields by wagon wheels. One day I was on one of those roads with Uncle Harm, heading to the mill on a wagon drawn by a team of horses. We were stopped by some horse-back soldiers. They asked if we had seen some of the soldiers with red-banded hats. We told them we hadn't and went on our way as they galloped off in quest of the "enemy" in red-banded hats.

Another day Uncle Harm and I were on our way to Allegan, the town eighteen miles south on a paved road. We passed by a large encampment of military tents where, for several weeks, they performed their maneuvers. That delighted Uncle Harm who had been in the military service in World War I. He pointed out to me that he had worn an identical uniform. One day he surprised sister Virginia and me when he came strutting out wearing that very uniform.

Uncle Harm taught me so many things—much more than how to plow with a horse team and how to drive the horse-drawn wagon. I turned a hand to milking cows and the other chores of farming, from hoeing corn, to helping with the harvest, hauling manure, and cleaning stalls. Uncle Harm did not have a tractor until 1968. A team of horses pulled the wagons, plows, and cultivators, helped by lots of manpower. Even after he owned a tractor, Harm kept his team for many tasks where they were better, such as navigating muddy roads. Harm would usually allow me to hold the reins because the team of horses walked in the grooved tracks and so the wagon rolled along so easily you could probably fall asleep, no harm done.

Once in a while an old Model T would slowly pass by the farm and Harm would say, "There goes Old Blind Garret." The distinctive chugging of the engine as he crested the hill alerted us that soon the clattering auto would come into view. Never once did I see Old Garret and had no idea where he was coming from or going to. I only had an image of him as a craggy old-timer with a long white beard. But I did notice that it was the worn-in tracks on the dirt road that steered the old Model T better than Old Garret ever could.

⌐

EVERY EVENING AUNT Grace joined Uncle Harm in milking their six cows. The buckets of milk were poured into a cream separator. When the handle was cranked, cream came out of one spigot and milk came out of the other. The cream was poured into milk cans for delivery to the creamery and the skim milk was fed to the pigs. The milk cans were submerged into a tank of cold water until they were ready for the creamery. The cows and horses were fed and that completed the evening chores.

After all chores were done, Uncle Harm took his "sit down" before dinner in his favorite chair. With his pipe stoked up and smoke curling up to the ceiling, he turned on the radio to listen to Gabriel Heatter give the war news. Everything we knew about the war in Europe was from the radio. Heatter seemed to start every broadcast in those days with these gloomy words, "There are dark clouds over Europe tonight…" so right away we were in a solemn mood.

⌐

SATURDAY NIGHTS WE dressed up and went to Burnips, the nearby village which would fill up with local farm families. While the women shopped in stores, the men gathered for conversation and to smoke their pipes. Kids got together for a good time and a break from isolation on the farm. Sometimes Uncle Harm would give me a nickel to buy a "paddle pop," chocolate-covered ice cream on a stick. If you were lucky, you would find the word "Free" burned into the stick underneath the ice cream. You could exchange the stick for another paddle pop or keep it for the next Saturday night.

Kids liked watching when someone bought gasoline from the tall pump outside the grocery store.The pump had a big clear glass tube at the top with lines marked on it showing the number of gallons you were buying. The grocer would come out and crank a handle and soon the glass tube would start filling to the mark showing the gallons you had paid for. Then a long hose with a nozzle on the end would let the gasoline run down into the tank of the car.

We never returned to Detroit until after thrashing time—that was the biggest event of the summer. Everyone always called it "thrashing" even though it was done with a "threshing machine." The excitement began when a huge tractor pulled into the driveway towing the large threshing machine with a dozens cars trailing behind carrying the teams of "volunteers," the neighbors who would help each other in turn with the task.

To a young boy's eyes, the threshing machine was like a monster with its moving belts, gears, pulleys and parts clicking, whirring, and clanging in rhythm. With each helper carrying out an assigned task, feeding bundles of wheat, oats, or barley onto a conveyor and with chopping blades devouring the crop, it was a grand scene to behold. Grain poured from the chutes and into sacks that the strongest and youngest farmers toted to the granary. We youngest kids took up prime spots in the grain bins and let the grain dump out on our feet.

There was fun and good spirits all around, but for the farmers, thrashing was very hard work. It had a special reward when it was over: a fabulous feast prepared by the women folk. There was chicken and dumplings, fresh-baked bread and pies, vegetables, potatoes and gravy. It might have surpassed a Thanksgiving dinner or maybe it seemed that way because all the hard work built up an appetite that made it taste so good.

When thrashing was complete, the big machine and the men moved on to another farm. The total operation lasted about a week, but for those involved it was a memory to last a lifetime.

At the time, I had no idea that those memories and those days in the country with Uncle Harm and Aunt Grace would be the reason that one day I would seek out and finally find my own paradise on my farm near Clarkston.

∼

BACK IN DETROIT for those elementary and junior high school years, there were many boys in the neighborhood to play games with, like Tag, Kick the Can, and baseball in the streets. Passing cars were rare so the street was our ball field.

We made our own toys. Inner tubes cut into rubber bands were used in wooden guns to use in a game of Tag. Bands cut from inner tubes also found their way into a popular toy—the slingshot made from a strong forked tree branch and a piece of leather. We nailed roller skates onto boards and made scooters. Many trips were made to the back of the grocery stores on Livernois to find crates we would knock apart and fashion into toys. We crafted kites from wood strips and newspapers. At the time we gave no thought to the lessons we were learning about creativity and resourcefulness that would serve us well in life's later challenges.

When I was a young boy I wore corduroy knickers and high-top boots. I was a young man before I wore long pants. I went to school with a pocket full of marbles to play before school and during recess. In winter you often had to duck snowballs thrown at you but just like any other time of the year, there were also chores you could do to make some money. I would take a snow shovel and knock on doors in the neighborhood and offer to clean the sidewalk for a dime. At the age of ten I sold *Liberty* magazines door to door. At age twelve I was finally old enough to have a paper route.

Dad loaned me the money to buy a newspaper delivery route on San Juan Street between Puritan Street and Six Mile Road. I picked up papers at a substation where we rolled and bagged them. I stood them upright in my bicycle handlebar basket so I could quickly grab one as I pedaled along the side-walk. While slowly pedaling my bike, with practice I could hit the porch—usually. But on occasion the paper would land in the bushes and I'd have to retrieve it and deliver it by hand. Daily editions of the newspaper were three cents each and the fat Sunday edition was a dime. It took a lot of effort to earn those seven to eight dollars a week. To deliver those Sunday editions onto peoples' doorsteps early in the morning, I had to leave home while it was still dark, even before the earliest robins were out for their breakfast worms. I would hear the robins' morning songs as I made my rounds. It is a memory as sweet today as it was when I was that young boy delivering newspapers.

Setting pins at the Roll-A-While Bowling Alley was much more financially productive. And it was indoors, out of the weather. For a men's league, I got ten cents a line. I did not like setting pins for the women's league as they bowled much slower. Another downside was that it was back-breaking work to earn those three dollars a night.

Working at the bowling alley was tiring, but once I got my driver's license, with those three dollars, I could fill the tank at eighteen cents a gallon and take a girl on a date and treat her to a nickel Coke and a dime hamburger.

In high school the girls wore bobby socks and loafers as did the boys. Pants were tapered and narrowed at the ankles. A popular haircut was the "New Yorker" brush cut on top with long sides combed back to form a "ducktail." Frank Sinatra was the rage, so bow ties were a fad.

I was twelve years old in 1941 when the war started. The draft took all eligible men and jobs became plentiful and materials became scarce. Rubber, gasoline, metals, sugar, meats, and many other items were in short supply and were rationed. Everyone was issued a ration book with little stamps you had to have to buy these items. It was important and patriotic not to throw away anything that might be useful in the war effort. I was in the Boy Scouts and worked with the other kids in my troop to collect aluminum pans and other metals. During blackouts we walked the street looking for house lights that might have been carelessly left on. But then, our patrol leaders were drafted into the military and our troop had to be disbanded.

The war decimated the neighborhood of all young men aged eighteen and older. My best friend's brother was killed in the invasion of Sicily. My neighbor, Doug Marsh, was in the Navy and aboard two different ships that were torpedoed and sunk.

No citizen escaped sacrifice for the war effort. Housewives saved the fat residue from cooking which was collected and used in the manufacture of munitions. Students were encouraged to purchase War Savings Bonds. At schools we paid for a twenty-five dollar bond on installments to the school. It was a patriotic duty for all to participate.

There were severe shortages of many items and so they were rationed. Ration books with coupons for certain items were allotted to each person and these were necessary to purchase those items in short supply. Gasoline, in particular, required stamps A, B, or C according to the distance to be traveled from home to work; C stamps were for commercial use. The sparse allotment left nothing for leisure driving, so many astute car owners used public transportation and would sell their precious coupons. The speed limit during war years was thirty-five miles per hour which deterred driving long distances. New tires were not available, so used tires were recapped and sometimes the new treads separated. That meant that spare tires, tire-patching and tire-changing tools had to be kept handy.

One of our rare lengthy trips during the war years was to Grand Rapids. Before the federal highway system, the route to Grand Rapids from the Detroit area was Grand River Avenue. That route passed through every town from Novi, through Brighton, Howell, Williamston, Fowlerville, and Webberville. It took an hour just to get through Lansing traffic, so the trip to Grand Rapids took about eight hours.

One evening while driving through Webberville, Dad was stopped by a sheriff. In that town, they did not issue tickets, but instead took you to the house of the local judge or magistrate where you paid your fine—in cash. Dad was so angry that every time we went by that judge's house, Dad would honk the horn for a long, long time.

One summer gas was in short supply so my sister and I went to Grand Rapids by Greyhound bus. Our step-mother packed a lunch and it was a good thing she did because with all the stops the trip took about ten hours.

As the war went on, it spared no one, including the civilians on the "Home Front." What was not rationed was hard to come by. We were allowed two pairs of shoes per year. So one day, our step-mother took us by bus to Windsor, Canada where we could buy new shoes. We wore those shoes back to Detroit to avoid inspection by the Customs officers.

When I was fifteen, I got a job as a stock boy at the nearby Kroger store. Laundry soap was scarce and the shelves were often empty. One day I brought out a fresh supply to stock the shelves. No sooner had I started than there was a stampede of women rushing to seize a box. Butter was also scarce and most everybody used margarine as a substitute, one time or another, if not regularly.

Throughout those years there was a constant and overwhelming desire for peace, for a return to normal life. We certainly have not had a war since then that so directly affected the daily lives of all citizens. I continued to work at whatever jobs I could get while in junior high and on into high school. When I worked at a gas station, that job meant much more than just pumping gas. I washed the windshield, checked the oil, and put air in the tires. I fixed flat tires and did lube jobs on cars up on the hoist. Bulk oil was kept in quart bottles near the gas pumps. Besides servicing the gas pumps, my responsibilities included refilling the oil bottles from a fifty-five-gallon barrel.

In 1947 when I was eighteen, I graduated from Cooley High School. I had many jobs in the factories of Detroit, including at Ford Motor Company, Dodge Hamtramck Assembly Plant, Kelsey-Hayes Company, Cadillac Motor Car Division, and other plants or shops. I worked where there was work to be had.

But then, in 1950, when I was twenty-one, the Korean War started. When I was classified 1-A, I knew I would soon be called, so I joined the Air Force. My timing was lucky because as I prepared to report to Fort Wayne, my "Greetings..." from the Army arrived.

My first train and airplane rides were to Texas. After basic training at Lackland Air Force Base in Texas, I was sent by train to Biloxi, Mississippi for radar school. Then I was assigned to Atterbury Air Force Base in Columbus, Indiana, a reserve wing of the Indiana guard. I soon had my fill of whiners and unhappy campers. We lived in tents, each of which had eight beds and an oil stove. We made the long trek to the latrine wearing only towels, shuffling along in shower clogs.

One day I was down on the line—the landing runway— when a large cargo plane was landing. That was unusual as it was not one of our wing planes. A large door opened, and one by one they unloaded wounded soldiers on stretchers and wheelchairs. It was obvious these heavily bandaged men had been recently wounded during fierce battles in Korea. We stood in silent awe. The war was now reality to me as I thought, "those poor guys." I thought about how insulated we were from that terrible conflict and about how unaware people were of the consequences of war. I wished others could also see and feel the pain of that sight.

We spent the winter in our tents until finally in the spring we got orders to report to Fort Benning, Georgia. There I was assigned to the 434th troop carrier wing at Lawson Air Force Base on Fort Benning. We were there to service the radar and radios on C-46 troop carrier planes.

I had the rank of sergeant and was in charge of six planes. Every morning I would enter the planes and check radio transmission with the control tower. I would sign a status log book to indicate for the pilots that the plane was either "O.K. for Flight," or "Grounded for Repair." We were on duty un- til about five o'clock before going to the mess hall for dinner. *Taps* was at seven o'clock and we were required to stand at at- tention and salute while the bugle blared over the loudspeak- ers. The music played on a well-used record and you would first hear a scratching hiss for a while before the solemn sound of the bugle. When the scratchy noise started, there would be a mad dash as we ran for cover because everyone wanted to avoid having to stand at attention while *Taps* played on.

It was only later that I learned how much of a bubble we were in at Fort Benning. While most people were worried about whether the Korean War would explode into a major

conflict with China or Russia, we were almost completely ig-
norant of world news. Sure, we knew the reason we were in
the military service was because our nation's leaders believed
it was in the interest of the United States to have forces in
Korea. But we didn't get newspapers and some of us didn't
get much mail from home. What little we knew about current
events was mostly sports news.

So none of us knew what might happen next. Would we be
sent overseas? We never really thought about that and just focused on whatever was our responsibility and the job at hand.
While civilians might be concerned the United States could
get drawn into a possible worldwide conflict again, we just
went about performing our own assignments. And my assignment was servicing those six C-46 aircraft.

That's what I was doing right up to the time President
Dwight D. Eisenhower made the decisions and took the steps
that led to the signing of a treaty with North Korea. Just like
that, the war was over.

Very quickly, we were offered early release with honorable
discharge. In October 1953, about a month before I was offered early release, I had a notice of my promotion to staff sergeant. Delighted, I sewed my new stripe on my uniform. But
that gave me pause. Now I realized I had to choose between
staying in military service with an increase in pay or a return
to civilian life. I thought about it. And about how this decision
would greatly determine my future. I was not unhappy or un-
comfortable with military life, but I decided to decline promotion to staff sergeant. Instead I took honorable discharge and
returned home to Detroit.

I was determined not to return to the factory floor, but instead would pursue a job as a draftsman. The G.I. Bill for veterans made that possible and there were many trade schools
available for those who had done military service.

I took a tool-engineering course that taught die design. The course was so easy for me they asked me to be an instructor. I didn't expect the transition from a military life to a civilian life and career would happen rapidly, but very quickly the die was cast.

Before long, another instructor offered me an even better job at a die shop where he was manager. I was happy to have a job that paid me a living wage. I had no idea that the day would come when I would no longer be working for a paycheck but instead would be my own boss.

⌐⌐

FOR MORE THAN fifteen years, until 1968, I designed dies at job shops. Then, a fellow designer convinced me we should start our own company. Soon we had contracts from Budd Company and Ford Motor Company.

We had the expected ups and downs for a small startup company dealing with economic conditions over which we had no control. In 1975 my partner said he had other opportunities and wanted to sell his interest in the company. That was fine with me, so I bought him out and became sole owner.

Now I had my own company, but like other suppliers to automotive companies and other industrial and manufacturing clients, as the economy softened I had many slow periods without work. But even if we didn't have projects in-house, I was obliged to spend days at the shop and to be available whenever something came up no matter the time. It was obvious that I needed to create work and find something I could market to the auto industry.

What I needed was a product that would either shorten manufacturing time, reduce cost to the consumer, or improve quality—and preferably all three. I set those as my goals: efficiency, economy, and quality. Then I had my *Eureka!* moment. It struck me that a revolutionary press loader would be very appealing to Ford Motor Company. I set to work making that idea a reality.

I progressed from making a sketch to a cardboard and thumbtacks mockup. Then, with my drawings and my bank book, I went to a small machine shop and had them build a prototype. Next I turned to an employee who had knowledge and experience with electrical circuitry and had him wire the necessary controls. The result was that I had created a working prototype that produced positive solutions to a long-standing problem in the manufacturing process.

The next step was to set up my prototype press loader and conduct a demonstration in front of client personnel in a position to make a decision—or at least a strong recommendation—for a purchase. We invited managers from Ford that I knew from my design work for them.

It was a pivotal moment and the demonstration went perfectly. A well-placed manager told me he would find an application for our system at Ford's Dearborn Stamping Plant. The demonstration had been a big success.

Once the system was installed and fully operating, it doubled production. That was the first big installation at Ford of such a system, a breakthrough that led to more installations and ultimately made it feasible for me to establish my own manufacturing plants. The system met all my three goals of efficiency, economy, and quality and although the customer was very pleased, the Union was upset. They called my machine "Otto," referring to the name of the worker it had replaced, while the worker named Otto was re-assigned to another press.

Those were busy times on several fronts, but along the way, I continued to develop other concepts to improve manufacturing operations and, as a result, I obtained twenty-four patents.

Success in business had its obvious rewards, of course, but the work was exhausting. Pressure and worry over-powered the ability to relax and enjoy a normal life. Over time, I was haunted with a worrisome question I played over and over in my mind: How do I get off this merry-go-round and start living a normal life again? My accountant had warned me, "Don't let the tail wag the dog."

It took a while, but eventually I managed to extricate myself and return to the simple life I had enjoyed in the country in my boyhood days in the post-Depression years.

IT'S BEEN MORE than twenty years since I rekindled my enjoyment of farm life. I spend my time as I please, as when I share Monday morning coffee at Brioni Cafe in Clarkston with friends who stimulate and enlighten me with insights from their very different backgrounds and life experiences. I'm grateful that in return, I am able to introduce them to a new (and very old) experience on the twenty-acre woodlot on my farm I call Sugarbush Manor.

In the country, every season has its share of the predictable and the unexpected. The calendar is of little use in telling us when the winter will at last yield its hold on the land. One year it may be sooner, the next year later, but inevitably life will stir below the ground in that brief weather window between winter and spring. In sugar maple trees, a life-bringing liquid will begin to rise, overcoming both cold and gravity. It is then that we tap the trees for a portion of their sap, as has been done in North America for more than three centuries.

In our specially fabricated cooker, we boil the maple sap, stoking the blazing fire to evaporate the water in the sap until we have a pure and sweet syrup. In this simple ritual with nature, we enjoy the companionship of good friends and the long-awaited transition from winter to early spring in Michigan.

I have also found a new adventure in learning about the roots of another kind of tree—my family tree. A quest into genealogy opened a doorway into the past as I learned for the first time about some of my ancestors. I continue my search into my family roots, digging deeper from the scant information provided by relatives in Ohio. It has been an amazing journey. After locating distant cousins who had family tree information, I traveled to Maryland to delve even deeper about my forebears. What began in curiosity became an absorbing quest for ever more knowledge about my family tree.

My hope for my descendants is that they find as much enjoyment in the simple things in life as I still do in the early morning song of the robin, a melody unchanged from those days I made my rounds as a youngster delivering newspapers.

2

FROM THE SAND HILLS OF NEBRASKA TO AN OAKLAND COUNTY BENCH
by Jerry McNally

"We shall not cease from exploration and the end of all our exploring will be to arrive where we started and know the place for the first time."

T.S. Eliot,
Four Quartets

MY DAD AND mom are from the Black Hills of South Dakota, more precisely from the Lead-Deadwood area of South Dakota. Gold mining was the engine for the economy and when that collapsed they moved to Detroit with their two children in 1925. They chose Detroit because my mom had an uncle living in Detroit. My dad was a plumber and things went well until the stock market crash of 1929 and the resulting Great Depression.

My grandfather had homesteaded some land in Nebraska. My dad had a choice: either join the bread lines in Detroit, sell apples on the street, or try his luck farming in Nebraska. My dad threw his tools in the back of his Model T Ford pick-up truck and headed west to Nebraska. He was joined later by my mom and their five children.

I came into my family on the eastern edge of the Nebraska Sand Hills on December 3, 1931. When I joined my family at birth I was greeted by two very unwelcome visitors. The two visitors came wearing long black canvas "all-weather" coats and big slouchy hats. The two visitors did not appear to be evil but they did appear to be totally without humor, feeling or goodwill. They were the walking dead. They appeared to be grim messengers of some great evil and disaster. They were the Great Depression and the Dust Bowl. They walked with me for the first sixteen years of my life.

The Depression was not unique to the Midwest—it was nationwide and even global. However, the Dust Bowl was unique to the mid-section of this country. The Dust Bowl has been described as the nation's greatest environmental disaster. John Steinbeck gave voice to those who fled the Dust Bowl in his masterpiece, *The Grapes of Wrath*.

I will walk with the these two companions of misery—the Dust Bowl and the Great Depression—who greeted me at my birth. I will walk with these constant companions for the first sixteen years of my life. They are the canvas upon which I will draw the high points and low points of my life.

Everyone who lived in north central Nebraska in the 1930s shared the same Dust Bowl weather. Everyone there also lived under the same bleak economic cloud of the Great Depression. However, my family was much less prepared than others to withstand the impacts of these two forces.

Neither Dad nor Mom had any experience with farming or ranching. This lack of experience was reflected in many ways. One example only: any visit to a typical farm or ranch would be heralded by a symphony from small farm animals, most notably, a flock of noisy geese, much better watchdogs than a dog. Several ducks would chime in along with the geese, and up would saunter a large friendly dog, tail wagging, tongue flapping, in quest of a handout. Clucking chickens would wander in from the vegetable garden, pecking at whatever in the scrubby grass and gravel. A fat grunting pig would be on duty for garbage disposal in preparation for its ultimate destiny of feeding the farm family. But had you visited our house you would be left wondering if anyone was at home for all you would hear was the wind, that lonely wind, hushing through the cottonwood trees. There were no small farm animals, no vegetable gardens at the McNally place.

In addition to the Great Depression and the Dust Bowl, three additional influences were constantly present. When I was born in 1931, it was the pre-FDR era, just prior to the New Deal and all of the New Deal legislation. At that time there was an unspoken assumption that if you were wealthy it was a sign of God's love and if you were poor it was a sign of God's disfavor. Compare that to the atmosphere in those days, for example, in Ann Arbor, Michigan where you could easily live off the land. Prior to the "New Deal" if you had nothing you had just what you deserved—it was God's will. The poor person did not do bad things, he was bad. So, being poor was the first powerful influence.

The second constant influence derived from the fact that my dad knew nothing about farming or ranching. He was a plumber-carpenter and house fixer-upper. On many occasions he proved that he knew nothing about farming and nothing about ranching.

The third constant influence was that I never knew my mom to be physically well. I always remember my mom as getting around the house by holding onto a counter or table. Shortly after my brother was born in 1936 she went to bed and never got up. She died in 1948 from multiple sclerosis.

My dad had built the family home out of cement blocks. It

was large enough but largely unfinished. We had no plumbing or electricity. We had a wood stove for cooking and heating. We burned cottonwood or poplar in the stove—it yielded lots of smoke and ash, but little heat and gave off a very unpleasant smell. I remember going to bed in the attic and waking up to see a small drift of snow in the middle of the bed. Frequently there would be a thin layer of ice on the kitchen water bucket.

I was the sixth child in a family of seven. My next older brother Jim was eighteen months older than I. When Jim started school I was three years old. Shortly after everyone but me headed off to school I would start asking "when is Jim coming home?" After a couple of weeks of this a neighbor suggested to my mom that she solve the problem by sending me off to school at age three.

The school, District 192 Holt County Nebraska, was two miles from our home. It went from first to eighth grade. Generally, there were five to eight kids in the entire school. It was a one-room school with a small barn for kids who had the luxury of a horse or pony. It had separate out-houses for boys and girls. It was a long walk to school, but I did not mind. The walk was across an unfenced field so there were no bulls to worry about. A farm or ranch is a dangerous place and a bull is a big contributor to that danger.

When I was three or four years old we were hit by a winter blizzard that can only be described as biblical. Snow drifted around the house to at least ten feet high, way over the doors and first floor windows. The wind and snow swirled around the house, shaking the doors and windows.

Our survival was at stake, so my dad moved everyone into the basement where there were fewer windows and no doors so there was less heat loss. For seventeen days, the entire family huddled together around a wood-burning furnace in one basement room.

In a second basement room we had two newborn calves and perhaps twenty newborn lambs. There is nothing cuter than a friendly and mischievous newborn calf. The calves and lambs were bottle fed. The lambs would cry like newborn babies and so the basement sounded like a nursery.

After seventeen days the storm broke and we emerged from our underground dwelling. Storms such as this were not that uncommon; however, this one was especially severe. It was common to have a wire between the house and the well and between the house and barn so that in case of a "white out," the wire would guide you to your destination.

Weather could be severe in other seasons as well. Sometimes the sky would be filled with swirling dust and then a quick rain shower would create a rain of mud. On one occasion our next-door neighbor had his cows bunched up along a fence line when a tornado came through. Many bolts of lightning struck the ground and most of his herd was electrocuted.

Our family did not fit into the culture of the Sand Hills of Nebraska during the Dust Bowl and Depression. We didn't fit in because we had no idea what we were doing. I cannot fault my dad for not knowing how to garden or raise chickens for meat and eggs. We simply were not in a position to be neighborly because our food situation was at best desperate. Not only was my dad a fish out of water but my mom was even in a worse position because of her M.S. condition and lack of farm experience. Our situation on the farm generated a lot of toxic shame in the entire family. My oldest and youngest brothers made some very poor life choices because of this toxic shame.

When we first moved to Nebraska in 1931 my dad tried farming for several years. He had to give it up because of the lack of rain and because bad land management across the region had caused the Dust Bowl. He then tried raising cattle. We ended up with about sixty cows. Each cow would give birth to a calf every year, generally in the early spring. These calves would be sold in the fall and this was our cash crop.

In 1937 a lifesaving event occurred. My Uncle Bill, an old bootlegger from prohibition, came to live with us, bringing his knowledge of small farm animals, gardening know-how, and a battery-operated radio. We would remove the battery from the car, bring the battery into the house and hook it up to the radio to listen to *The Lone Ranger* and some sports shows. The only artificial light that we had was provided by a kerosene lamp and lantern, one of the reasons that life on the farm is "early to bed and early to rise." Uncle Bill's arrival was a watershed moment for my family as we now could produce more of our own food.

⟋

THE NEBRASKA FARM was my grandfather's homestead. Following World War I, my Dad had homesteaded land in Wyoming. He felt that he had to go to Wyoming and assert his ownership rights, otherwise the neighbors would claim his land through a process called adverse possession. So he homesteaded a section of land, 640 acres, in Wyoming and in 1939, when I was eight years old, my Dad, brother Bob and I drove to Wyoming to assert those rights.

This was prior to World War II, long before the expressway system and chains of motels and fast food places. Travel by car was very slow and lodging was limited to hotels and tourist homes, which were a precursor to bed and breakfast places. One place we stayed was in Chadron, Nebraska in a tourist cabin; it was a place I would later liken unto a migrant worker's cabin from John Steinbeck's *The Grapes of Wrath*. The rate was the princely sum of one dollar for the three of us, including a community shower. In those days, there were no children—youngsters were just small adults.

When we arrived at the Wyoming land, my principle job was cook and dishwasher, so one evening I went out to the creek to get some water. This creek was normally dry, but when it rained, small basins in the creek bed would fill with water and generally last until the next storm. As I knelt to fill my bucket with water, I sensed something. Then, I heard a rattling sound just as I saw, a couple feet from my right foot, the coiled rattlesnake. It didn't take me long to get back to the cabin and for Dad to get rid of the snake.

Over the next weeks, I kept a sharp eye out for rattlers as we fenced a good portion of the section, cut and stacked hay and thereby asserted our ownership of the land. That part of the country was so vast and unpopulated that it could be many miles between signs of civilization, let alone a town or city. For us to go to attend Mass on Sunday we had to drive sixty miles each way, looping through corners of three states: Wyoming, South Dakota and Montana.

⟿

IN 1945, ANOTHER major milestone occurred, the death of President Franklin Roosevelt. President Roosevelt had given us reason to hope. Upon hearing of FDR's death, an old man stood in the middle of the street crying. A reporter asked the old man if he knew FDR and the old man replied "No, but FDR knew me."

In the spring of 1945, when I was fourteen, my dad, brother Jim and I were living on the farm. We sold off the livestock and whatever farm equipment we had and joined my mom, sister and two brothers in Detroit. During the Depression and Dust Bowl the going wage for a man was a dollar a day. I can remember my oldest brother working for thirty-five cents a day and my dad worked with two teams of horses for twenty-one cents per hour. If men were desperate they would work in exchange for a portion of food and a place to sleep in the barn with the livestock. This arrangement was called "choring for food."

I did learn from my farm experience in Nebraska how much joy there is in the so-called "little things in life." Seventy-five years later it is a great thrill after waking up in the morning to go out into the hallway and adjust the dial on a little device called a thermostat and command all the heat and cool air that you want. No more knocking the snow off some frozen slabs of wood. It is a thrill to go into the bathroom and get all the hot and cold water that you want, not to mention the luxury of an indoor toilet. The same joy awaits you when you enter the kitchen. The timer has been set on the coffee maker so the coffee is ready. You reach into the refrigerator and freezer for food you can prepare on the electric or gas stove. Of course you flip on the TV or radio to get the sports news or the weather report. A big difference compared to trying to start a fire with wet or frozen wood.

My dad, brother Jim and I arrived back in Detroit in the spring of 1945. I was ready for the tenth grade. At that time it was important to get into a Catholic school. We found an opening at St. James in Ferndale. St. James was a typical small, co-ed, parish high school. My three years at St. James would have been typical had it not been for my mom's illness. She was totally confined to her bed and wheel chair. My mom died in the spring of 1948, the same spring that I graduated from high school.

When I graduated I was sixteen and too young to find employment in Detroit, but my family had a contact in Blair, Nebraska, a town thirty miles north of Omaha. There, an electrical contractor offered me a job that I had until I joined the

Air Force in December of 1950. As it happened, my two and a half years in Blair, Nebraska were well spent because it was there I learned the electrical trade. That knowledge and experience gave me well-paying jobs in the Air Force and all of those summers during undergraduate and law school.

As part of my tour of duty with the U.S. Air Force, I spent thirteen months in Thule, Greenland, about eight hundred miles north of the Arctic Circle. There, the calendar year is four months of total darkness, four months of total sunlight, and four months of transition.

During the so-called winter months, there was little snow and temperatures would range between twenty and thirty below zero. The buildings were elevated off the ground so the permafrost would not be thawed and cause the structures to sink. The buildings we lived in were kind of reverse refrigerators, keeping heat in and cold out. Constructing the Air Base at Thule was a monumental project that, given the bitter weather, has been compared to the building of the Panama Canal.

Water for drinking, shaving and showering had to be delivered by truck and pumped into a storage tank. After those uses, that water was then drained into a second storage tank and used to flush toilets before cycling into a third storage tank to be hauled away by truck.

My job was to operate and maintain the electricity-generating systems, something for which my experiences in Nebraska had prepared me.

The expression, "the middle of nowhere," might well have been coined to describe the Thule base. There was no town nearby with restaurant food, so the only alternative to the awful mess hall food was the occasional "care package" from home.

It was a long year in Thule, but there was a bright side and it opened up a door for me to advanced education. The University of Maryland had started an extension program there and I was able to start college and earn six hours of college credit.

～

WHEN I GOT out of the Air Force at the beginning of 1954 I enrolled at a small Catholic college in Missouri. This college was essentially a preparatory school for a Catholic seminary. During my college years I was introduced to the three great Greek philosophers—Socrates, Plato and Aristotle. In a way, Greek philosophy gave me an alternative route from my otherwise unpromising life because that introduction to Greek philosophy was really the beginning of my formal education.

When I was in law school, electrical work was slow in Detroit so I found work in Denver, Colorado for one summer and in Minneapolis, Minnesota for another summer. But as for summer jobs, the best was the very last. Right before I started in law school I got a job on a Great Lakes ore carrier called the *J.L. Durston*.

The *Durston* was one of the older ships on the Great Lakes, built around 1912. It had a capacity of 8,000 tons of iron ore, coal, flax seed or whatever it might be carrying. It had a crew of twenty-eight men and operated 24/7.

The food on the ship was outstanding—a crew member could have steak three times a day, if he wanted to. However, any type of alcoholic beverage was strictly forbidden.

On a few occasions we would deliver coal to Duluth, Minnesota or Buffalo, New York but our principal route was hauling iron ore from the Upper Peninsula to Cleveland, Ohio. The round trip between the U.P. and Cleveland would take seven days. On one occasion we were crossing Lake Erie on our way to Cleveland and a freakish storm blew up. The surface of Lake Erie was as flat as a table top even though the winds were blowing around sixty miles an hour. The wind must have been blowing in a slightly downward direction to keep the lake so flat. Frequently the wind would form water spouts, a column of water two to three feet in diameter and twenty to fifty feet high. The wind would hold this column of water upright for a few seconds then collapse it only to form another water spout. This type of storm had to be unusual because when we arrived in Cleveland, a veteran sailor expressed his amazement. There, two tug boats—one at the bow of the *Durston* and one at the stern—would take us up the Cuyahoga River. Tug boat assistance was necessary because the river was very narrow with one curve after another in the seven miles to our destination.

Upon returning, before we reentered Lake Erie, we would pick up coal to burn in the ship's boilers. We would stop at the coal dock and two huge mechanical-like hands would pick up a train car of coal and dump it down a chute into the ship's hold.

My job on the *Durston* in 1960 was well before any environmental protection or consciousness. The seven miles of the Cuyahoga River was completely lined with factories or manufacturing plants. As we were being towed up the river one could see all kinds of industrial waste being dumped into the water. Yellow, red, brown fluids poured out of large pipes and into the river. Occasionally the river would catch fire and burn so hot and so long that it would put the safety of the steel bridges at risk.

When we unloaded iron ore in Cleveland, a small boat, probably thirty feet long, would pull up alongside the *Durston* and sell all kinds of toilet articles and beer. This was called the "bum boat." If someone spent too much time on the "bum boat" he would need assistance just to make it back onto the *Durston*.

There was a silly little mimeographed newsletter that circulated among the ships sailing the Great Lakes. On one occasion the headline for the newsletter read something like: "An ore carrier fired the bed bug." An interesting headline, so I read on. It turned out that some ships had a crew member whose job it was to maintain the officers' quarters. This person was called the "bed bug" and this particular bed bug referred to in the headline had been fired. Mystery solved.

Poets and other romantic types often describe how beautiful and breathtaking sunsets can be; however, while on the ship, I found the dawn to be more gorgeous and breathtaking than the sunset. The dawn often starts out with a thin red or yellow line just above the horizon through which the sun peeks before the horizon explodes into a canvas of dramatic color.

I had been on the *J. L. Durston* for five or six weeks and the union steward had continued to pressure me to join the Seafarers International Union. The initial union dues were around five hundred dollars. My plan was to start law school that September. I had a choice: to join the union and postpone law school or leave the ship and go to law school. I chose the latter.

～

I HAD BEEN a law student at the University of Michigan only one month when I experienced one of life's rare indelible moments—to see a future president make a challenge that would have incalculable consequences, not only domestically, but also worldwide.

It was 1960 and seldom has the nation been so captivated by a political figure as it was when John F. Kennedy ran for president against Richard Nixon. Much of that passion had its origins in the struggles of citizens of Irish descent for full participation in American society. For decades, Irish-Americans sought opportunity in politics. Kennedy emerged as the perfect candidate—a war hero, a charismatic U.S. senator with a beautiful wife, and an Irish Catholic.

On October 14, 1960, when Kennedy visited the Ann Arbor campus of University of Michigan, he was greeted as a rock star. Along with hundreds of other students there, I expected him to arrive at about 9 p.m. It was a cool, wet night, but the crowd was still good-sized when he showed up at 2 a.m. He said later that he was amazed anyone had waited around that long for him.

Kennedy stood on the steps of the Michigan Union and spoke less than five minutes, but his opening remark endeared him to his audience: "I want to express my thanks to you, as a graduate of the Michigan of the East, Harvard University."

But it was a challenge he gave Michigan students that night that had truly lasting impact:

How many of you who are going to be doctors are willing to spend your days in Ghana? Technicians or engineers, how many of you are willing to work in the Foreign Service and spend your lives traveling around the world? On your willingness to do that, not merely to serve one year or two years in the service, but on your willingness to contribute part of your life to this country, I think will depend the answer whether a free society can compete. I think it can! And I think Americans are willing to contribute. But the effort must be far greater than we have ever made in the past.

And thus was born The Peace Corps.

That was quite an introduction for me to the University of Michigan where law school would prove to be challenging and interesting. In addition to my classes, I had two part-time jobs. One was as a playground supervisor for an elementary school in Ann Arbor for only one hour a day. The other was as a part-time kitchen helper at the Veterans Administration hospital in Ann Arbor.

⁓

WHEN I GRADUATED in 1963, legal work was somewhat scarce so I did electrical work while I waited for my results on the bar exam. I helped remodel a bank building in downtown Detroit.

My first legal job was assistant corporate counsel in the City of Dearborn. I was somewhat embarrassed by Mayor Orville Hubbard's racial position but I knew this would be only a temporary job. At the time I took the job with the City of Dearborn, I did not appreciate what a great opportunity it was. My boss, Ralph Guy, was considered one of the top one hundred attorneys in the entire country. He later became a Federal Court of Appeals Judge. The next stop for Ralph would be the U.S. Supreme Court.

When I was with the City of Dearborn I was single. I had some extra time so I got a night school part-time job teaching philosophy at the University of Detroit, a job I kept for ten years.

I was with the City of Dearborn Legal Department from 1964 to 1965. The Lyndon Johnson Democratic landslide of 1964 gave me an opportunity in the Oakland County Prosecutor's Office. The Prosecutor's Office was now staffed with Democratic Party appointees and there were lots of opportunities to try serious felony cases. I was with the Prosecutor's Office for just one year when I joined a solo-practitioner in his law practice in 1967. I stayed with the practice of law until 1969 when I was elected District Judge.

The District Court is in the lowest court in Michigan which means it is the court closest to the people. Everything comes into the District Court, from dog bite cases to first-degree murder cases. All crimes must filter through District Court.

All legal cases are significant, especially to the participants involved, but some cases have more broad and lasting consequences to society than others.

The Kevorkian case was certainly one of my significant cases. It is an understatement to say that Dr. Jack Kevorkian had given a lot of thought to the freedom to die. Social forces are a great influence on the developing legal system. Modern medicine was steadily becoming so effective that people with Alzheimer's disease and cancer were living beyond a life span at a desirable quality of life. Some people could simply not bear going on with life due to severe pain or the over-powering feeling of indignity. They wanted the freedom to choose to end their own life.

The "right-to-die movement" was going underground where it could avoid the prohibitions of our legal system. For example, a sixty-five year-old old woman visits a doctor's office and describes her situation to the doctor: "My mother is ninety years old and has lived with my husband and me for five years. Her cancer has spread to her spine and brain. She is in constant pain and every day begs God to take her and relieve her suffering."

The doctor explains that he has some new pain medicine that is very effective. However, the mother is to take not more than one pill a day. To take two or more pills a day would certainly kill the mother. The doctor tells the daughter he is giving her a thirty-day supply but she must not give her mother more than one per day.

The next day, the daughter calls the doctor in a near panic and tells him, "I put the thirty-day supply on my mother's night stand with instructions to not take more than one per day. I counted the remaining pills and there were only twenty-five left. Mother must have taken five pills at once and now she isn't responding." End of life. End of story.

It was to deal with situations such as this—and to use such cases to elevate the issue to national prominence—that Dr. Kevorkian developed what the media called his "suicide machine." He called it the "Thanatron," which he said was from the Greek, for "the peaceful death machine." To build his machines, Dr. Kevorkian went to flea markets and yard sales for parts, and from a junk yard he got timers from washing machines. The timers were actually very simple mechanical devices providing the desired amount of minutes for washing, rinsing and spin drying cycles, just what the doctor ordered.

For each "assist," Dr. Kevorkian adjusted the mechanical timer to provide for so many minutes of a saline solution, so many minutes of a barbiturate and so many minutes of potassium chloride. Dr. Kevorkian would hook the patient up to an IV, then the patient would start the timing device. It was of crucial importance that the patient start the device because the last operative actor is the person responsible for the subsequent results. Dr. Kevorkian would always make it clear that the patient could change his/her mind at any time before the suicide machine got into the last cycle. Dr. Kevorkian performed this procedure more than one hundred times before he dealt with Thomas Hyde, his last patient, who had ALS or Lou Gehrig's disease. Hyde was so frail and crippled he was unable to turn the knob on the washing machine timer to start the process and so Kevorkian started the cycle himself. Because Dr. Kevorkian himself started the entire process—a fact clearly shown on a video recording that Kevorkian himself had insisted be made—his action caused the death of the patient. That exposed Dr. Kevorkian to the murder charge. He foolishly represented himself at trial and was convicted. He was sent to prison and served nearly all of his sentence before being released early because of his own terminal cancer condition.

Judges deal with quite a range of cases, some involving significant potential liability, such as one case I had in which the liability of General Motors was at issue.

When a new vehicle built by General Motors is damaged in shipping, whether by railroad or by a car carrier truck, an assessment is made of the damage, then a decision is made whether the vehicle should be repaired or relegated to the scrap heap by cutting the vehicle up. If the damage is minor or limited to sheet metal, it would probably be repaired and sold as new. If the damage to sheet metal is serious or the engine or drive train is damaged, it would probably be ordered destroyed. General Motors does not want the liability of selling damaged vehicles.

The man whose job it was to take these seriously damaged vehicles to the junk yard for destruction saw an opportunity. He wanted to make a few bucks by saving several otherwise apparently new vehicles from the car smasher. He took home with him several vehicles that were marked "to be destroyed." He sold one to a friend for a very modest price along with the directions: "Never take this vehicle on a public highway. It does not exist." The unique identifying "vin" number had been removed.

Predictably, the buyer took the vehicle onto a highway and—no surprise—had an accident. The sheriff arrived and gathered all the accident information. The sheriff at first concluded that the vehicle did not exist but then reconsidered and said it required further investigation. His inquiries revealed the full story and the seller of the vehicle was charged with "Receiving stolen property worth more than one hundred dollars."

I dismissed all charges, ruling that General Motors had abandoned the property as worthless when they ordered it destroyed. What impressed (or depressed) me most about the case was the incompetence of G.M. employees. No one appeared capable or willing to take responsibility for ordering that a given vehicle be repaired or destroyed.

❧

NOT ALL CASES involve huge corporations or any potential high monetary stakes, but any time a person appears in a court of law, it is indelibly important to that person. The "Case of the Clarkston 88" is a case in point.

Super Bowl parties have long since become a national pastime across the country, an integral part of the hoopla surrounding the football game itself. Clarkston is no exception, although in the early years of Super Bowl mania, gambling was not as accepted and tolerated by the legal establishment as it seems to have become.

In the early 1970s, an enterprising local bartender rented the American Legion Hall on M-15, just north of Clarkston to host his own version of a Super Bowl party. His ambitious concept featured an admission ticket for a hundred dollars to cover all manner of goodies. In addition to viewing the football game on several large-screen television sets, there was ample food and drink and, not incidentally, the gamut of gambling options, including roulette, cards, and dice games.

While that party was going on, my wife Carol and I were at a much more sedate little gathering, the typical kind that featured nothing more daring than one of those big grids of a hundred squares you could take a flyer on for two-bits.

Meanwhile, the notorious "Clarkston 88" party at the Legion Hall was in full swing when uninvited guests—the Michigan State Police—put in an appearance. They showed up with a bus to convey the eighty-eight party-goers on a complimentary ride to the Oakland County jail.

The Oakland County prosecutor promptly phoned me and asked what he should do with these several dozen presumed wrong-doers. I told him to release everyone on a signature bond with a court appearance for the next day, a Monday.

That Sunday evening, to better prepare myself for the hearing, I read the eighty-eight names—it read like the "Who's Who of Clarkston." There were several police officers, attorneys, elected officials and many prominent local citizens. I began to form in my mind what I would tell them when they showed up the next morning.

There was no doubt that a gambling conviction would have been a disaster on a person's record, especially many of those with prominence in the community. So I could sense that there was considerable relief when I told them they could earn a dismissal of the charges if they paid a modest fine and had no gambling violations during the next six months. I suppose you can say I cautioned them to "go forth and sin no more."

I don't recall a single one of them appearing again in my court.

The story merited a front-page article in *The New York Times* and earned the participants a place in local folklore in the "Case of the Clarkston 88."

Among the most unusual cases that came to my court were a couple that involved dog-fighting. As I learned from court testimony, the arrangements to stage this particular illegal activity are often necessarily temporary and made on very short notice. In the cases I dealt with, the sponsors found a location and quickly set up an octagon-shaped fighting pen about four feet high made of four by eight sheets of plywood, sort of like a small boxing ring.

Dog-fighting is illegal in all fifty states, but in some places it is a much more sophisticated activity with more permanent fourteen-by-twenty pits. Fights can last just a few minutes or several hours, and both animals may suffer injuries including puncture wounds, lacerations, blood loss, crushing injuries and broken bones. Although fights are not usually to the death, many dogs succumb to their injuries later, and losing dogs are often brutally executed as part of the "sport."

The dogs involved are anything but Lassie or Fido scrapping in the back yard. There are several breeds used, each of which is deemed the ultimate fighting dog by its adherents or breeders. Some are bred for one reason only—to fight another dog of the same breed.

Why would anyone want to be involved in such a horrific spectacle? Blood lust is part of it. Perhaps the stronger motive is that betting is substantial and dynamic—bets are made and changed during the fight, which seldom lasts more than four minutes. The owner can throw in the towel for his dog at any time.

Beyond the brutality in the event itself, since dog fighting is an illegal activity, it attracts a criminal culture that leads to other crimes, so I presided over these cases with severity.

~

LOOKING BACK TO when I started law school in 1960, I thought I could just walk away from the harshness of my very early life. I imagined I might start again with a new identity, sort of like the federal witness protection program where an informant gets a whole new identity including plastic surgery, a job, a place to live, and some income. No surprise that I learned that things don't work that way and I came to realize that I had to go back and reclaim my growing-up years.

Carol and I married on September 11, 1965. We have four children, three boys and one girl. Our children were a big incentive for me to reconnect with my roots.

The popular expression "It is not the destination but the

journey that is important" certainly applies to marriage. I compare marriage to a walking journey from Michigan to California. On a journey like that you will encounter all kinds of weather, all kinds of people, and all kinds of fortune. You meet different people and walk with them for a while and then separate and encounter other people. In marriage you don't have to begin every conversation with "once up on a time." You can begin in the middle of the story. In 2015, Carol and I celebrated our fiftieth wedding anniversary with a gathering with our family and then we followed that with a three-week trip around California.

⌐

THE MICHIGAN CONSTITUTION states that a person over age seventy cannot run for judicial office. He/she may finish a term after reaching that age but may not run again. When my last term expired I was seventy-one.

I've been retired since 2002 and the last fourteen years have been most worthwhile. The psychiatrist and author R.D. Laing compares retirement to the biblical Prodigal Son parable:

You are born into your father's house. You leave. You make your way in life. When you retire, you return to meet the "yourself" of that early life. You get to know yourself as if for the first time.

The celebrations as described in the Bible's parable of the Prodigal Son await you when, at last, you retire to yourself.

One can think deep thoughts about good Karma or bad Karma. For me, looking back on those days in the Great Depression and the Dust Bowl of Nebraska, or the mornings when I watched the sunrise from a Great Lakes freighter, or the countless hours spent on the judicial bench, it is simpler to say that wherever I have been and whatever I have done, I have felt the hand of God in my life.

3

LIFE IS A BOTTOMLESS BUCKET LIST
by Carole Cotter Bodner

"We were paid a penny a bunch, and a bunch was ten onions. One lady regularly made twelve dollars—that's twelve hundred bunches of ten onions each, working all day. I didn't last long at that job."

L IFE WAS GOOD until one windy spring night in 1948 when the elm tree came crashing down.

It drove half our picket fence into the soft ground and along the way it turned my swings and monkey bars into a gnarled mess of twisted metal. Daddy had attached swings and monkey bars to that eighty-year-old elm tree and now it was down, taking my swing set and monkey bars with it.

We had moved into our new house across the street from Balduck Park on Detroit's east side to have more room after my brother Allan was born. Housing had been frozen during the war, so my parents had stayed in their tiny attic apartment in Detroit even after I was born in 1943.

My mother, brother Allan, and I spent a whole day watching men with loud chain saws slice large round slabs off the fallen tree. Daddy spent whatever time he could over the next week, using those huge wooden circles to mark the trail from the front gate to the back yard. Getting my swing set rebuilt took until July Fourth. Digging out the broken picket fence, painting and replanting it took until Thanksgiving.

It was a good thing there was other stuff to do in our neighborhood. We had a sidewalk for roller skating and the park had a great sledding hill. We had a sandbox next to the vegetable garden behind the garage. And twelve kids lived on our block, so the Cotter yard was very popular.

In 1950, Daddy's job as a draftsman at Briggs Manufacturing was scheduled to move to Sterling so we moved to Big Beaver Road in Troy Township, which would become the city of Troy, Michigan. There, everything was different. We had almost eight acres with a woods and a creek in back of the property. Eventually there were eight big willow trees separating the house and lawn from "the farm," all of which came from one four-foot willow branch my mother's childhood friend had brought as a housewarming gift.

For the first five years in our Big Beaver home, my mother's father often stayed with us, and he helped build a two-car garage with breezeway to the house. Detroit was undergoing a great deal of "urban renewal," and many loads of lumber were dumped behind our new garage, and Grandpa removed nails and screws, and stacked the cleaned lumber. He and my dad built a corn crib, a greenhouse, and a doghouse for our beagle, Spot. A big project was the two barns they built, one for geese, ducks and chickens, and a second one for the tractor, lawnmower and tools, because we finally had a second car. There was always something being constructed, something in the works, and whenever the cement truck arrived, neighbors came to help while the concrete was being poured and leveled. When a structure was going up, neighbors would help lift up and hold the assembled walls while another person screwed the nuts onto bolts that held the wall tight to the concrete floor. Some stayed to help lift roofing materials, and even to help finish the roof when they could see rain coming.

Most of those neighbors were older than my parents and that meant there were no other children nearby to play with. During elementary school, I didn't miss having kids my own age, but during high school years it would have been nice.

Most neighbors had gardens and also raised chickens, ducks or pigs. Neighbors also introduced us to new foods, such as white peaches, quince, red and black raspberries, and red currants. There were snap pea pods, asparagus, rhubarb, and yellow and beefsteak tomatoes. Sometimes we would have pheasant and smelt and from the neighbors at the mushroom house we had pizza, mushrooms, plum tomatoes, garlic and basil. We traded fruit (we had a whole acre of strawberries), vegetables, and eggs with neighbors, the milkman, and the mailman.

Even back in the early days when my parents lived in Detroit, my mother and a neighbor shared bushels of cucumbers and peaches to can. In Big Beaver, neighbors often were invited to bring a pot and pick whatever was ripe. Our milkman, Don Flynn, lived on Big Beaver Road four miles away, so my mother would drive our tractor—with Allan and me in the trailer—to pick apples, apricots, and cherries. On Good Fridays (the full moon), our friend, Mr. Corey, would go across to Canada and then down to Point Pelee south of Windsor, Ontario to dip smelt. Mama would give him a tub for us and he would bring it back with hundreds of the little fish. It became an Easter tradition to clean the smelt and stack them in empty milk cartons for the freezer. Fish heads, guts and roe were buried in the garden, because we had no trash or garbage pickup. That freezer was the first new appliance my parents ever bought, and it was a necessity in our household. Almost everything from then on was preserved frozen, except for tomatoes, quince, pears and grape jelly which we canned.

～

ON THE INSIDE of the front and back covers of this book, there is a montage of images from the early days of the authors. One of those images is from a 1951 photograph of my father standing in our driveway, leaning against Mr. Dawson's Ford tractor. Behind them on two-lane Big Beaver Road, a lone car whizzes by. That picture must have been taken on a Sunday because Big Beaver Road had traffic only on weekday mornings and evenings as men went to work and returned home. Otherwise it was perfectly safe and a common sight for a tractor to chug along at ten miles an hour as no family had a second car, and the nearest Martin Lines bus stop was a half mile away, at Kleitch's Grocery on Rochester Road. The traffic load was so predictable that a policeman was assigned to be at the corner of Coolidge and Big Beaver Roads from 5:00 to 6:30 each weekday evening to control traffic while Mr. Brooks' milk herd left their pasture and orchard, and crossed Big Beaver to spend the night in the barn behind Mr. Brooks' house. If no policeman was at the corner, drivers parked at the road and helped stop traffic for the crossing cows. In 1970 Mr. Brooks' entire farm became K-Mart World Headquarters.

I know when that photograph was taken, Mr. Dawson was telling my dad how Mrs. Dawson was convalescing. A few weeks earlier, the missus had been running the tractor and dismounted to move something aside. The tractor rolled on, pinning her beneath it and breaking her right arm and leg. The mailman was passing by and happened to see her, and so he drove his car directly into the field, loaded her into the back seat, and rushed to the hospital six miles away, above the Cunningham's Drug Store in Royal Oak.

Had the mailman not glanced into the field as he made his rounds, no one would have been around until the end of the day. Such "farm accidents" were not uncommon in the country and some were serious if not fatal. Mrs. Dawson was still agile after she healed, but didn't spend much time on the tractor after that. From then on, my parents, Allan, and I turned off the tractor and set the brake whenever we disembarked.

My first paying job was cleaning and bunching scallions (green onions) for market at Mr. Yannich's truck farm, where Telly's Nursery would one day be located, north of Big Beaver Road on John R. The truck farm bordered on the same woods as our farm. We were paid a penny a bunch, and a bunch was ten onions. One lady regularly made twelve dollars—that's twelve hundred bunches of ten onions each, working all day. I didn't last long at that job.

My first non-paying job was folding and forming boxes that mushrooms are packed in. That was my mother's idea of a way my brother Allan and I would show what good citizens and neighbors we were. When the mushrooms were ready to harvest, everyone would work eighteen-hour days at the mushroom house to get the mushrooms to market right away. They had to be harvested while the gills were still tightly closed, keeping moisture in the cap so they would weigh the most. Our task of forming boxes saved time at a critical point in the process.

⌒

WHEN I WAS in sixth grade, I was ill most of the school year. There was not a lot to do, so I listened to the radio every weekday. Soon, I was hooked on *Pepper Young's Family* and *Lorenzo Jones*. In those days, people knew who sponsored radio shows—kids would sing the advertising jingles or say the tag lines the way the announcers did. *Pepper Young* was sponsored by Beech-Nut Gum and Camay, "the soap of beautiful women." *Lorenzo Jones* was sponsored by Procter & Gamble, the company that created the long-running institution of the afternoon "soap opera" and sponsored many serials.

After I was well, I went back to school where I quickly caught mumps. I again had to stay home several weeks, but this time, Lorenzo—a would-be inventor who was always getting into some scrape or other—was no longer on the air and so I never knew how he got out of his last predicament. That left me with a lifelong strong avoidance of cliffhangers.

As I recuperated, in addition to keeping up with soap operas and doing my schoolwork, I worked on a To-Do list. These were the things I thought longingly about doing when I finally got well. At the time, I had no idea that I had invented my own "bucket list."

Some of my goals had target dates:

—By age fourteen: Ride a bike
—By age fifteen: Drive the tractor
—By age sixteen: Have a driver's license
—By age twenty: Be able to eat brownies with the walnuts
—By age twenty-five: Buy a new car
—By age twenty-five: Be able to eat onion soup and drink wine and beer (without a grimace).

Some of my goals had no target dates:
—Travel to Europe and Australia
—Visit all forty-eight of the United States
—Sail in the Chesapeake Bay
—Live in Washington, D.C.; San Francisco; London, England; or Sydney, Australia.

ᕗ

IT WOULD BE a few years before home air conditioning gravitated to the north where only restaurants and stores routinely had it until the 1970s. So on hot summer days, we went to the water to cool down. Throughout my childhood and into high school days, there had been many opportunities for swimming beginning with when we lived in Detroit. Then we had gone to Belle Isle and swam in the Detroit River, or travelled on July Fourth to Ontario's Point Pelee to swim in Lake Erie. A good time for that was July Fourth because there were only Americans enjoying a holiday, as Canadians had already had their holiday on July First.

Three or four times a year, a boat ride on the Detroit River was just the thing to cool down. Most of the time we got off the boat at Bob Lo Island (also called Bois Blanc, like several other islands in the Great Lakes). Sometimes we took advantage of the carnival rides and Dodge-em cars but usually we stayed on the boat back to Detroit because that was where the cool was. On the walk from the last bus stop to the foot of Woodward where we caught the boat, we stopped at Vernor's for ginger ale where my favorite was "cream ale," ginger ale with two squirts of cream in a tall glass. That was something you could never make at home quite like they did at the counter.

When we moved to Big Beaver in 1950, the neighbors told us that one of the best places to go swimming was the Salt Water Swimming Pool. So we would walk a half mile west to Rochester Road, then take the Martin Lines bus north to Long Lake Road. The water there was crystal clean but cold, so sometimes we would drive north on Rochester Road ten miles to the end of the road, at Lakeville where the lake water was not as clean but also not so cold. We also swam in lakes in Oxford, Lake Orion, and Waterford and in Troy gravel pits now known as Emerald Lake and Lake Charnwood.

During the 1950s, Metropolitan Beach was developed, with a mini golf course and swimming, on Lake St. Clair, and that made for an easy ten-mile drive due east on Big Beaver Road, now Metropolitan Parkway.

There were lots of other things to do, places to go in the area. Years earlier, on the last day of elementary school, everyone in Big Beaver Elementary went on a picnic to Bloomer State Park where John R ends north of Avon Road in Rochester Hills. A railroad track ran through part of the property, so we sometimes left pennies on the track so the train wheels would flatten them. If the weather was good, there would be softball games all afternoon; if the weather was bad, we cooked hamburgers in the pavilion fireplace, then played board games. The park had polio warning signs at the creek, a common reminder in those days.

When I was in the eleventh grade, Thunderbird Bowling Lanes was built and on Saturdays, Troy school children could learn to bowl for a special rate. It was so popular that whole families came on weekends and high school students came on the Fridays there wasn't a football or basketball game. Some of the kids would go over to Woodward Avenue for cruising but I only did that once, ending up at Ted's Trailer near Square Lake Road with Norman Dollar, Diane Hildebrant, and Lloyd Klusendorf for hot chocolate and french-fried onion rings.

During my last two high school years, I was a counter girl at Troy Cleaners on Rochester Road just south of Big Beaver Road, where a Burger King now stands, and worked at Clawson Cleaners and Avon Cleaners.

～

IN THE 1950s, the Cold War with Russia was a daily fact of life in America. 1953-54, Senator Joseph McCarthy, a Republican representing Wisconsin, vaulted himself to prominence with claims he never substantiated that there were many communists in the U.S. Department of State and in America's universities. He himself was later censured for his tactics which gave rise to the term "McCarthyism" for fear-mongering.

While I didn't feel personally affected, my mother and her siblings—given their Slovenian heritage—did not want to call attention to themselves or appear "foreign." On the streetcar or bus, or even in a restaurant or store, they would speak only in English. Mama's family, who lived in Hamtramck, owned acreage on Dequindre Road, between Wattles and Long Lake Roads and on weekends would attend events at a nearby park popular with "Carpathians" where everyone attending spoke some Slavic dialect. Mama said that these were strictly social and cultural events, but because of the Cold War tensions and McCarthy's red-baiting, everyone was too afraid to continue the gatherings, squelching immigrants' connections to their heritage. Not until the Russians launched Sputnik was it considered not only permissible but actually nifty to know a Slavic tongue.

~

A FEW YEARS later, as a high school senior taking a required course in government, I tried to pay attention to the 1960 presidential campaigns of John F. Kennedy and Richard M. Nixon. Since I would vote for the first time in the next presidential election (in 1964), I thought I should know the candidates' stances on important issues. It was not easy because nothing was simple and much on television was a lot of noise. What did appeal to me was that Nixon seemed "experienced" and Kennedy had announced a "Peace Corps" while on a visit to the University of Michigan campus in Ann Arbor—that was exciting. But I did not form an educated opinion that would point to whom I would vote for. Later, when I watched the inauguration on television, with Kennedy in formal attire and hatless, I remembered Eisenhower in his brown homburg and business suit taking that same oath and was stunned that this *should* be a dressy occasion. Then I heard Kennedy's inaugural address and felt that this would be a more exciting administration than any I had known.

During the Detroit Riots of 1967, I was living in Ann Arbor. At night, looking to the east toward Detroit, the sky was brighter than it should be, so we knew there were fires. We worried that rioting would spread to other Michigan cities. How would all this upheaval stop? In 1963, when I had traveled in Europe, I heard that the same things happened there, too, but were not so publicized. Back in Michigan, in 1968, the Detroit Tigers won the World Series for the first time since 1945, proving there is nothing like focusing on the local winning team to bring a city together.

⁓

FAST-FORWARD TO my 50th high school reunion. That was when it became clear to me that I needed a new bucket list.

I still cannot ride a bicycle. That is unchanged, even though a friend donated her bike so my boyfriend at the time could attach adult training wheels as a gift for me on my fiftieth birthday. While the wheels were attached, I could bike the trails around Arlington and Alexandria, Virginia, but that is as close I have been to properly riding a bike.

As for driving the tractor, I did indeed earn the right to check that one off when I was twelve and Big Beaver Road was still a sedate two-lane country road. Things had changed remarkably by 1970 when I left Michigan to work in Ohio, Virginia, and California. By then, Big Beaver Road was no place to be driving a tractor.

Another check mark for getting the driver's license by age sixteen—I managed that during Thanksgiving weekend that year.

I hit a couple more at age sixteen during a visit to Ann Arbor for high school "Senior Day at Michigan." The onion soup, as it happened, was an easy one, and after lunch I ate the dessert brownie, complete with walnuts—in no way was I going to let anyone know that I was a fussy eater. Since then, of course, I go out of my way to have walnuts in brownies, breads, cake, fudge, and ice cream.

At twenty-four I bought a new 1968 slant-six Plymouth Valiant. It was practical, not an elegant or show-off car, but, then, I am a girl, so that is OK. I also bought snow tires— which I changed myself twice each year. I also changed the engine oil and replaced two burned-out headlights. I was not independent, but these are all chores that I cannot do on my car today (steel-belted radials are significantly heavier than 1960's tires, and much more "stuff" has been shoehorned under the hood).

~

ALSO, AT AGE twenty-four I took advantage of a student flight to Europe, and, thanks to no drinking fountains in all of Europe, came back with a taste for beer, wine, coffee, and tea. To reinforce my experience with wine, I took a six-session wine-tasting course so that I would at least have the vocabulary to describe and remember what wines I really liked. During the first session I discovered that my preference would no longer be sweet reds, and that, if I did not initially like the taste of a wine, tasting food with the wine usually made the wine palatable. I had a truly wonderful week cramming for the sixth session "final exam" (wine identification and essay questions).

The student flight was cheap, $250 roundtrip Detroit to

London, leaving in mid-June and returning Labor Day. Following advice in *Europe on 5 Dollars a Day*, I joined American Youth Hostels; that was my ticket to free admission at almost all museums in Europe, and overnight accommodation at youth hotels and hostels for as little as twenty-five cents a night and never over a dollar. Student hotels offer just a bunk bed, with no limits on when you enter or leave; hostels have a schedule, and doors are locked at 9:00 p.m., and unlocked at 9:00 or 10:00 the next morning after all the listed clean-up chores have been completed.

Most hostels also once had a different life; I have overnighted at a castle with a dry moat in Rothenberg, Germany, and in a WWII bomb shelter in Vienna, Austria. Neither country was on my bucket list, but I was hitchhiking with my girlfriend from the University of Michigan, Larri Short, and one rule she and I learned early was to travel the longest distance on any ride offered. Larri and I and a German student we had met at breakfast were offered a ride from Amsterdam to Frankfurt by a student who spent his vacation returning rental vehicles to other cities. Along the way he mentioned that he was actually returning the car to Salzburg, Austria and Larri and I decided to stay on past Frankfurt to Salzburg.

My goal on this ten-week trip was to visit as many places as possible, and that would help me decide on which cities or countries I wanted to spend more time on future trips, and which cities or countries I could check of my list. Stuttgart was the only city I did not like; I decided I needed to return for a second look around all the countries—England, Ireland, Wales, Netherlands, Austria, Switzerland, Italy, Germany, and France.

~

By 1969 I had been teaching school longer than I had ever thought I would. I still yearned to see other places, to travel often, and to live in several places outside of Michigan, so I needed a job that was more like a craft that would allow me to be a gypsy. The want ads in Detroit newspapers listed columns of openings for computer programmers, and so did newspapers from New York, Washington, D.C., and San Francisco. I wasn't familiar with computers, and didn't know how programmers did whatever they did, but it seemed that everyone everywhere wanted one, so I wanted to be one. I had heard that many companies were training their own programmers, so I wrote to IBM, General Electric, Booz Allen Hamilton, Honeywell, Chevrolet, and K-Mart. Only Booz Allen responded "after you have some training, contact us." All the others invited me to an interview, and IBM and General Electric sent me to Virginia and Maryland for additional interviews and testing. Since I had been a teacher for several years, all of them saw me as a courseware designer (teaching via computer), which was new then in 1969. But, no job offers came.

After taking the Federal Service Entrance Exam (Civil Service), an interviewer from the Air Force Logistics Command at Wright-Patterson Air Force Base in Dayton, Ohio, offered me a job in their computer programmer trainee class starting in July 1970, after my current teaching job finished for the year. The six-month training course on all five different computer systems used in Air Force Logistics was more comprehensive than any school could have offered. I attended class from 8:00 a.m. to 5:00 p.m. and did programming homework until after midnight every workday, because it was due at 8:00 a.m. the next day. After graduating, I would owe the Air Force a commitment of two years.

I had fully intended to work my two years, then look for work as a contract computer programmer, living the gypsy life I'd looked forward to, but I kept getting promotions and really interesting projects, and I really liked designing, developing, and testing programs and systems. I spent the first four months of 1974 working at Hill Air Force Base in Utah testing software programs developed by other people in my office at Wright-Patterson. While I was head of the Air Force Institute of Technology Civil Engineering School computer systems department, I was caught in a reduction-in-force (laid-off), but promptly was hired by the Navy ADP Selection Office (ADP-SO) in Washington, D.C. and moved there in June, 1976, just in time for all the bicentennial events. ADPSO was the office that acquired almost all computer and telecommunications equipment, software, and services for the Navy and Marines. It's all men.

I was very lucky to be in that office because I was now in the company of people rungs above me on the career ladder, who had worked for all the big computer companies, and all were personal friends of the living "famous" people in the computer world. Plus, I was assigned a mentor who knew, and had the respect of, everyone in computer acquisition.

And, I was living in Arlington, Virginia, and had one more check for that bucket list!

⁓

SEVERAL FRIENDS IN the Washington, D.C. area had sailboats, and they needed crew. When I was a member of American Youth Hostels (which I had joined to stay in European youth hostels), I took a sailing course in Michigan, but never did any other sailing, so I looked forward to developing some sailing skills. Because most of the sailboats were on the creeks and rivers that feed the Chesapeake Bay, I could check off another bucket list item.

During 1977 I sailed every weekend (Friday night to Sunday evening) from May until Thanksgiving. I had the best tan ever, but in December my great tan faded to yellow, and the bridge of my nose sported my first wrinkle. Sunblock SPF15 came on the market in 1979, so until then I wore long sleeves and a big hat when sailing.

The Chesapeake Bay has a soft, oozy bottom, perfect for clams, oysters, and crabs. While sailing in the shallow areas away from the freighter lanes, everyone aboard would watch for the floating markers signifying crab pots. In the twenty or so years that I sailed, we caught a crab pot only once, and had to jump into the water to release it from the boat's propeller. Although the water could be inviting on a hot, muggy day, we never swam in the Chesapeake because of the jellyfish. The Chesapeake is a brackish mix of salty ocean water in a predominantly fresh water river. Whenever there is heavy runoff from the fresh water rivers and creeks, the salinity decreases and the jellyfish multiply and cluster in groups that look like whipped egg white. They are called sea nettles because you cannot see the long tentacles with poison stingers.

A really wonderful part of sailing is sleeping on the deck under the stars. The field of stars is denser and the stars are brighter over the water and there is little man-made light fading the view. Every night would be different because no two creeks offer the same sounds, or landscape or morning birds. When weather was cold or rainy, we would raft-up (tie to another boat, preferably one with a coal-burning fireplace for heat) and share food, schnapps, and stories. After forty-eight hours completely away from my work life, I was refreshed, and could start the workweek with a great attitude.

⌒

IN 1979, I married a Marine who was stationed in Twentynine Palms, California. After a half year of a bicoastal marriage, I got a teleprocessing job in San Diego with the Navy. I was still living alone, but was now only a two-hour drive away from my husband. I lived and worked on North Island, and moved in on New Year's Eve, 1979. Flowers were blooming everywhere. The azaleas were perfect and it was December. The poinsettias were six feet tall. The jacaranda tree in my back yard was in full bloom with hanging purple-blue and lavender blooms like pearl necklaces.

I started a vegetable garden in February—then the rains came. In one night the slugs ate everything in my front and back gardens. When I turned on the outdoor lights, I could see those varmints almost to the top of the garage and house walls where they spent the day. There is a zinger in every paradise.

And then there was the fog. Some mornings it was so dense that I couldn't walk from the front door to the sidewalk without first touching the ground to know if I was on the sidewalk.

Because hostages had been taken in Iran in November 1979, trees on North Island had yellow ribbons around their trunks. On Sundays, people would roller skate all over the island and neighbor ladies would be out in golf carts to shop because there was no traffic. From my perspective on the San Diego side of the island, airplanes seemed to be landing amidst city buildings. On the ocean side of the island was the old and famous Hotel del Coronado with its fabulous beach and views.

I experienced another glitch in paradise one night when my first earthquake shook my basset hound Molly awake and she did her best to run for safety. I already knew that standing or walking are almost impossible during an earthquake, but perhaps it was Molly's first earthquake too, because she slipped and struggled as she tried to get to the bed.

When a job vacancy was announced in Twentynine Palms, I applied and was hired. Unfortunately, I worked with my husband, and too much togetherness did not help our relationship. When we divorced, I immediately landed a great job using all the programming and computer acquisition skills I had acquired on all my past jobs. I worked for the Navy in Alameda, California, across the bay from San Francisco. Another check mark for the bucket list!

AFTER SEVERAL REALLY great years of living in Northern California, I was ready to go back to the Washington, D.C. area (living in California was expensive), and had my pick of several jobs with people I had worked with who had moved to other agencies and computer manufacturers, and were now hiring. Because I had handled projects implementing system software conversion to new computers, I joined the Federal Conversion Center in Falls Church, Virginia—and joined old friends in new jobs.

I also joined a sailing club, and sailed in a wider variety of boats in the Chesapeake, Virgin Islands, and Greece.

Along the way I met Steve Bodner, who also sailed, canoed, hiked, and camped, and was a birdwatcher. We canoed the Boundary Waters Canoe Area (Minnesota and Ontario) twice. We married in 1998 in Michigan, where we each had a mother and brother for witnesses. Then we started looking for a retirement home in Michigan and Virginia, not really ready to leave the milder winters of the mid-Atlantic, but wanting to be closer to family. When we retired in November 2001, we were ready to rejoin our families in Michigan. The attack of 9/11/2001 sharpened our definition of "home."

In 2002 we moved into my mother's basement in Troy, Michigan, while we house hunted, keeping in mind the drive to both mothers' homes. We needed a large house, as Steve had five siblings who would visit often, and we needed to plan that if a mother became ill she could stay with us and have her own bed and bath. So, the Clarkston five-bedroom, four-bathroom house we found was perfect, and was on a small lake with no motors, perfect for canoe and kayak.

Two years later, in 2004, Steve died from lung cancer.

⁓

BY 2007, I had completed Master Composter and Master Gardener training and was looking for a place to perform the obligated forty hours of volunteer work. Bittersweet Farm Community Garden in Clarkston, just two miles from my house, driveway to driveway, was perfect.

Bittersweet Farm, owned by Bob McGowan and his wife Barbara Hamilton, is part of a 150-year-old former dairy farm. The purpose of the garden is to provide the Gleaners food bank in Pontiac with seasonal produce that Gleaners then distributes to churches and soup kitchens throughout southeastern Michigan. We deliver about 3,500 pounds annually of cucumbers, summer and winter squashes, beans, beets, tomatoes, peppers, Swiss chard, kale, collards, potatoes, turnips, onions, shallots, and herbs. I am currently the garden manager. I know that this volunteer-run garden is a worthwhile use of my time so I expect to be in the garden for a long time to come.

⁓

OVER THE YEARS, that seemingly bottomless bucket list was never far from mind. When I was a youngster traveling with my parents, I had been to most of the contiguous states, but in 1970, I still needed to visit all of New England and Minnesota. Thanks to Hawaii and Alaska joining the union as states, my goal then became "all fifty of the United States." During the last two weeks of June 1970, before I started working at

Wright-Patterson AFB, a friend and I drove all over the six New England states and were delighted to have no real traffic because the summer season there starts in July. We had no crowds, and the summer rates had not yet gone into effect. Cape Cod was delightful, and the driver could look around, too, and see the sights and the countryside. All the seafood had a flavor I had not ever tasted before; I decided that must be the taste of the sea, which does not stay with the food after freezing.

After spending the early winter of 1974-75 in the Utah mountains, I decided to spend some of the rest of the winter in a warmer climate so I vacationed in Hawaii during January 1975. That left me with just two states to go!

While working in the ADP Selection Office I needed to travel to observe computer benchmark tests before awarding a contract. Minnesota is the home of more than one computer manufacturer. So, by November 1978, I had visited all forty-eight states of my original bucket list entry.

I don't yet have plans to visit Alaska, which would be my 50th state. If I do plan to visit the South Pacific, I think that I would rather see New Zealand. From what I have heard about the land of the Kiwis, it could prove to be a full bucket list all by itself.

4

GOING ANYWHERE...DOING ANYTHING... THEN COMING HOME AGAIN
by Wally Niezguski

"Under the wide and starry sky
Dig the grave and let me lie:
Glad did I live and gladly die,
And I laid me down with a will.

This be the verse you 'grave for me:
Here he lies where he long'd to be;
Home is the sailor, home from the sea,
And the hunter home from the hill."

Robert Louis Stevenson
Requiem

IN 1934, MY father decided that any job would be better than working in the iron ore mines in Michigan's Upper Peninsula. So that year, at age 17, he came to Detroit where his first job was—you might say, a big step up—washing windows on the Fisher Building. He got the job working in maintenance under my Uncle George who was married to my father's sister Sophie who is 101 years old at this writing.

My parents met at Sloppy Joe's Tavern on Eleven Mile Road in Royal Oak Township. In 1941, they married and moved to Ferndale where I was born in March 1943, just before my father left for World War II.

During the War years, my mother and I lived in Hazel Park with her Scottish-born parents. Grandfather Scotty drove a horse-drawn cart to deliver milk and on two memorable occasions I saw him come home in that milk wagon, drawn by his hat-wearing horse. Grandfather Scotty would hold me with one arm while with the other he put the feed bag on the horse.

Although I was too young to remember the events as they were happening, years later I attended reunions of my father's shipmates and heard many stories about their experiences during the war. My father's ship had engine trouble on their way to England. Had that not happened my father would have been at the helm of a landing craft hauling thirty troops at a time to Normandy Beach where so many died. Instead his ship later sailed for the South Pacific where they were greeted warmly by some very hardened GIs because their ship was loaded with thousands of cases of Greasy Dick Beer from Ohio.

After my father returned from the War, he did what so many veterans did—bought a house on the GI Bill. Our new home was in Royal Oak Township which later became Madison Heights, an absolutely great time and a fine place to grow up. We didn't need expensive, store-bought games because we had kick-the-can, marbles, baseball, hide-and-seek, and whatever we could make up 'til the street lights came on and up and down the block moms were calling their kids in for supper.

Every man on that street was a returning War veteran and there was at least one youngster in every household. In 1949, when I was six years old, we were the first on our block to have a TV. Neighbor kids would gather on our front lawn to peer through our windows at the flickering black and white image on our ten-inch marvel of technology.

That fall, there was one bigger and older kid who often would chase me home from school. My father explained to me that the boy only chased me because he figured I wouldn't stand up to him. A few days later, it happened again but this time, as I got close to our house, I saw my father watching out the window. All in one motion, I stopped, turned, and swung and watched in shocked amazement as this big kid—a good head taller than me— landed flat on his backside. He got up holding his face and ran home. A few minutes later his father came running across the street and my father came out to meet him and let him know how it was going to be. Lesson learned: Don't go looking for trouble but never run away from a challenge.

I got a different sort of challenge from Sister Mary Dolereta's ruler. It all started with another boy throwing grapes at me. Just my luck—Sister Mary Dolereta looked up just as I threw one back at him. Now, I have no idea how much the good Sister weighed but, habit flowing behind her, she came down the aisle as big and as fast as a Mack truck and as she came she was flicking holy water in my direction. That is, right up until the instant she stepped on a grape and was transported heavenward in a billow of black and white robes. But gravity quickly took over and Sister hit the floor so hard that people came running up from the floor below to see whatever could have exploded. Sister Mary Dolereta was so upset she used a word that probably would have been quite familiar to one of my father's shipmates.

In 1955, when I was twelve years old, I was glad we had a television set because that summer I came down with rheumatic fever. My father put a bed by a corner window in the living room and that at least gave me a perfect view of the neighborhood. Many of the kids came to that window every day so even those times were not so bad and before long I was healthy again. In fact, in a few months I was strong enough that I could show off my young sister, Barbara, then about a year old. She must have trusted me a lot because she would stand upright on the palm of my hand with her knees locked and I would march around the house, holding her straight upright, giving her the perspective of being tall as she beamed with pride and excitement. Over the years I did this with other infants but none of them did it as well as Barbara.

~

I HAD ALREADY experienced one of life's turning points in the sixth grade. I discovered football. Not only that, I quickly could see that I was good at it. Football lesson No. 1: not a good idea to run with your tongue hanging out. I learned that one moment after someone hit me and I almost bit it off. The experience had its upside because I got my few minutes of local fame. All my friends wanted to see my stitched-up tongue, swollen like a wedge of raw beef. If only I had thought to charge for a look as my brother Larry did years later, collecting a quarter a gander after he smashed his face on a steering wheel.

I survived elementary school at Saint Mary Magdalen only to learn that my parents had decided I was going to a parochial high school—no further discussion on the subject. Or so they thought. Obviously they didn't know that I had heard that if you were not in attendance for the first day of class, you were out and your spot was given to the next kid on the waiting list. The timing was perfect for me because I knew I was going to be on vacation up north at my grandfather's cabin on the South Branch of the Au Sable where I had spent many days every summer.

So, just before I would have to be on hand for that important first day of school, knowing I had other fish to fry, I grabbed a tackle box and a rolled-up tent and took off into the woods. Everything went great—for the first few hours. I set up the tent and went off to catch some fish. Hours passed and I began to wonder if someone had moved my tent because I knew I couldn't be lost. Could I? Finally I spotted a strangely bent tree I recognized as being near my tent. I learned later that Native American tribes would bend a young sapling to use to mark a trail. Exhausted, I crawled into the tent and fell immediately to sleep until the next morning when I awoke to a vigorous shaking on my tent. I crawled out and looked up at two forest rangers.

As the rangers led me out of the woods, past one lake after another, they told me how worried my family was. The rangers finally got me back to their jeep and one of the rangers guessed rightly that I must be hungry because he handed me his lunch and a thermos of coffee. The cheese sandwich was delicious and so was the coffee, the first cup I had ever had.

I knew I had caused a lot of trouble and concern but as soon as my family saw me they were so relieved I never got the expected spanking. They knew I was sorry and ashamed, but they couldn't have known just how happy I was that I was now able to go to the public school where my friends went.

There was so much to do during those high school years. I wanted to make some money of my own, but my father wouldn't let me get a newspaper route of my own, so for a year I teamed up with Chico Jozwiak and helped out on his until I got accepted as a caddy at Red Run Golf Club. As often as I could, I carried double, lugging two heavy bags five miles in the summer sun to earn twelve dollars. Now with serious money in my pocket, I could afford two dollars for gasoline and a cruise up and down Woodward Avenue, hitting all the twenty or so drive-ins from the Totem Pole in Royal Oak to Ted's Trailer at Square Lake Road. It was neat watching people staring at our flashy cars. Sometimes we'd park and open up the hood, show off the chromed engine.

Most of my best buddies in high school caddied at Red Run and somehow most of us managed to scrape up enough money to get a used sports car or, for some guys, a muscle car. We'd get up a caravan to find the best winding roads where we could test our cars' suspension. We might go up to our favorite, Highway 119 between Petoskey and Cross Village, a road that winds in and out of forests and sand dunes. Sometimes we even went over into Canada. We were kids living out *American Graffiti* when that screenwriter was still just a kid pedaling a tricycle.

A favorite gathering place on Woodward Avenue was the parking lot for the strip mall in front of Royal Oak Beaumont hospital at Thirteen Mile Road. That is where I learned how to set the timing on my Austin-Healy and balance its dual carburetors that were so tricky to get humming in sync.

Depending on the time of year there were different destinations to hit. When we went to the Salt Water Swimming Pool north of Long Lake Road on Rochester Road on Saturdays in the summer, it seemed like half the people there were from my Madison High School. Or on other weekends we'd go to the amusement park and beach at Walled Lake, Cass Lake beach, or the apple orchards between Rochester and Lake Orion. There were hay rides out on Dequindre, Jack Scott's Dance Ranch, roller skating at Clawson's Ambassador Roller Skating Rink, and tobogganing at Bald Mountain. When the weather was bad, there were always the long matinees at the three movie theaters in Royal Oak.

But it wasn't all cruisin' and draggin'. Bigger for me were

sports. I loved getting the ball in football and averaged 9.8 yards per carry my senior year. Any kind of running was fine with me—even without a ball in my hands—and I placed second in the state regionals in the low hurdles. Still, I studied well enough that I managed to be the first in my family to graduate from high school. When Northwood opened its campus in Midland, I was offered an athletic scholarship. We had a good year but when their scholarship funds ran out, I had to move on. I didn't realize it at the time but that turned out to be a life-changing experience for me. It would lead to what would be the first of many forays to places I had never heard of.

In 1963, with the Northwood scholarships gone, I got recruited—along with two friends—to Western State in Gunniston, Colorado, the highest college in elevation in the country.

The first thing I did was climb to a mountain top and drink in the spectacular view. Once football season was over, I spent every weekend exploring, getting to know real cowboys, hunting, fishing, and skiing. Because I was a transfer, I had to sit out as a red shirt my first year and when I didn't get much playing action the next two seasons, I dropped out of school in spring of 1966.

Connections I had made at ski lodges led to a succession of jobs in the ski world, starting as a bartender at a lodge and eventually becoming manager of the cocktail lounge. I tried often to quit so I could spend more time on my college studies but every time the owner would add a new benefit I couldn't resist.

In March 1966 I had heard that Playboy was opening a club in Detroit so I sent a letter asking for an interview and citing my experience managing the cocktail lounge in Gunniston. Bingo. I was hired as a room director and given managerial training.

Many of my friends thought I had the greatest job in the world when I was manager of the Detroit Playboy Club. They didn't realize that I spent most of my waking hours there, arriving mid-afternoon and working straight through until three or four the next morning. And it was no easy job for the bunnies, either. It took a long time for the bunny mother to get them into their costumes, with the metal stays that accented their bosoms but prevented them from bending forward and making it necessary for them to do the "bunny dip" lest a body part come tumbling out. Everything the bunny did was stylized even to the extent of how they handled a shot glass while they poured the drink and the mix. The practices perfected at the original Playboy Club in Chicago were used in Detroit and every other club.

Would-be bunnies faced long odds—out of a hundred trying out, only ten were hired and maybe only one of those ever actually made it out on the penthouse floor. They had to deal with much that was unglamorous and follow to the letter many rigid rules on posture and behavior. It took so long to get into and out of costume that bathroom visits had to be greatly minimized. They had to urge customers to buy items with the Playboy logo and use their charms to increase their tips. They made great money even though they worked only four days a week.

It was strictly prohibited for bunnies to date customers or club employees, like me, so I actually became good friends with them, good enough that they nicknamed me "Captain Nice," maybe at least in part because they couldn't pronounce my last name. That nickname drew laughs from my friends when they came to the club and heard the bunnies call me that.

Part of my job was to do Penthouse Show announcements and introduce entertainment acts like Barbra Streisand, Larry

King, and Sammy Davis Jr. Other tasks weren't as enjoyable. I was told I had to be more hard-nosed, for example, and fire any bunny who was behaving improperly with a customer. That bothered me more and more and finally I gave the Club two weeks' notice and took a job with a wine distributor, covering the lower Gratiot Avenue territory.

The wine business was so good that I could hit all my accounts in time to take off on Fridays and go to ski shows where I worked for Heart Skis, as a rep with Bill Peterson. That not only tied into my wine sales job, it was also something I had liked doing since I had gotten into skiing in Colorado with Heart Ski. I traveled to Boston, Cleveland, and other cities manning a booth where I would meet people and invite them to private parties to push our products.

As always seemed to happen, in Fall 1966 something unexpected came along and once again I was on the move. A friend I hadn't seen in a while told me he had been in Alaska working on a fishing boat. His skipper was looking for another hand and so in late winter of 1967, I drove to Seattle where I sold my car to raise enough money to get me to Alaska and carry me through until salmon season started the first of June. I was in for a big surprise.

The first jolt came when I looked at the bill for my first breakfast in Anchorage: two eggs and toast, ten dollars, thank you very much. But there I was, so to bridge the couple months gap, I took a job bartending and that gave me enough time off that I got to do a few things, such as panning for gold in Homer, skiing at Mt. Alaska, and enjoying Mt. McKinley where you could see for two hundred miles, reminding me yet again of Colorado.

Soon enough it was time to get to Seward and board a seaplane to Kodiak Island to help ready the fishing boat, the motor vessel *Marylyn Rose*, a purse seiner. We loaded tons of gear, ropes, netting, cork lines, lead lines—enough stuff to fill a garage. There was a place for everything, but very little space to eat and sleep. Everyone on board was a partner earning a share of the season's catch, so nobody minded the long hours and tight quarters. Sometimes we stayed out five or six weeks at a time, steering clear of the rest of the fishing fleet. The *Marylyn Rose* was something of a magnet because Chick, our skipper, had been fishing these waters since he was eleven years old and the younger skippers would follow us wherever we went. We did our best to make that very difficult to do.

Sunday Law means no fishing from dusk Friday evening till dawn Monday morning. During that time, we would drop anchor in a bay or on the lee wind side of an island, spending Saturdays mending nets and making repairs. Weather permitting, on Sundays we might take the skiff and go ashore and do some beach combing.

To reach the mainland, we crossed the Shelikof Strait between Kodiak Island, a distance of about thirty nautical miles with powerful tides and swells up to thirty feet, not for the queasy.

Early season was for sockeye on the main coast, lasting the first half of June. Then we were back across the Strait to Kodiak Island for humpies or pink salmon until late August or early September, depending on success. If luck was poor, we might stay longer for king salmon and or dog salmon.

Putting the nearly three-quarters of a mile long net into the water and setting it had to be done again and again, forming a full circle with a purse line running through heavy brass rings to hold the net down about ninety feet deep. Pulling in this purse line with a power winch would close the bottom of the net creating a purse from which the salmon could not escape. Sometimes we would net only a couple dozen fish in a set. Other days we would fill our hull. Every day we would rendezvous with a cannery's tender ship to sell the day's catch and restock our supplies and that way we could stay out at sea for weeks at a time.

The work was hard regardless of how good the catches were and I looked forward to the lulls in action to enjoy the scenery and the beach combing and exploring. One Sunday I discovered an old abandoned village that I later learned had been wiped out by plague. It still had Russian literature on the walls and handmade furniture still in place. You could tell that bears had rummaged through the place. We always carried a .44 magnum hand gun and were on the lookout for Kodiak brown bear which can stand ten feet tall on hind legs.

That was the first of what would become more than half a dozen seasons and once a season was over, it was time to settle up and collect our shares. We were all partners in the enterprise, including the boat itself which got one share, plus another one and a half share for use of the boats' gear, and the skipper, who got two. Everyone shared in expenses for food, fuel, and supplies.

Some skippers would gear their vessels for the crab season but that wasn't for me and besides the *Marylyn Rose* was a little small for crab pots. Most fishermen earned enough during salmon season that they did not have to go crabbing. Those who did not have a good season for whatever reason might not have a choice and would re-gear their vessel with crab pots.

In Fall 1967, it was back to Seattle and this time I actually thought I might stay a while. I had in mind getting a job and using my off-work hours to explore that beautiful part of Washington and especially to poke around the fishing villages along the coast and the many islands in the Sound like Whidbey Island, now a highly popular destination. That soon became possible when I got hired at Boeing Aircraft as a quality control inspector working on the Boeing 737. I liked working for Boeing but didn't like the rush-hour drive in the rain every day and when the company wanted me to move to Mt. Vernon, an even longer drive, I knew it was time to leave.

It was late January 1969 with still some good skiing before the next fishing season so I headed for Crested Butte, Colorado, the ski area I most enjoyed to ski. I would ski almost every day and bartend or wait tables at night. With spring coming on I thought perhaps I would forgo Alaska by placing a bid for the riding stables owned by the ski area. The plan was to take groups of people over Maroon Bells, a range of mountains between Crested Butte and Aspen, a distance of about twenty-five miles as the crow flies but if the crow was on horseback it took all day. Still, it was an opportunity I couldn't resist. Although my bid didn't win I was offered the job of City Marshal, something I hadn't thought about but sounded interesting.

So that summer of 1969 I was sworn in and put on the badge. They gave me a blackjack and a .357 magnum but I was told I could load it only with .38 cartridges. With my gray policemen's shirt paired with a blue leather vest a friend made for me to pin my badge on, I looked more like someone out of the cast of *Death Valley Days*, complete with cowboy hat, jingling spurs on my boots. I might be seen riding a horse leading a parade down main street on the Fourth of July, directing traffic from horseback, or posing for family photos. I considered myself a peace officer—there would be no cutting off hippie's hair in this Marshal's town.

One day a report came in that a stack of lumber had been stolen—a serious heist in these parts. After some detective work, I had a prime suspect. I approached him and said flat out, "The owner knows it was you." I made him an offer he was smart not to refuse—that he go to the owner and 'fess up and he might just get let off the hook and be allowed to work off the money involved. That's just what happened and as a bonus he ended up with a job for some time afterwards.

During that summer I had heard about a friend who was building a 55-foot schooner in California and was in the final stages of the project. He offered me a job, my own bedroom, and great cooking by his wife Connie. It was an easy decision and since being the chief law enforcement officer wasn't a life-long ambition, I was off to Venice Beach, California late that fall of 1969.

My friend Fred was building his boat out of cement fur-row. His method was to build the vessel's shape out of wood upside down, applying three layers of chicken wire, one layer of steel rebar vertically and one horizontally forming a four-inch grid around the entire structure, and then another three layers of chicken wire all twisted together forming a cage which cement could be troweled or shot into. When all that was done, a crane was needed to turn the structure over. I watched Fred's knees wobbling and thought he was going to die when the cables slipped a couple of times with his boat swinging in the air. But somehow we both lived through it.

From that experience working on Fred's boat I got the idea to build my own purse seiner to take up to Alaska. With a ves-sel like that I could do very well for myself. I started looking into a place I could build the boat, and researched catalogs for designs. I found space available to build it in Venice Beach, a yard with a high wooden fenced area, enough space for maybe twenty boats to be built. Most of the materials I needed could be had close by.

I still had three months until salmon season began so I left on explorations to Mexico and quickly got some bad news—a Mexican National would have to own fifty-one percent of the boat. But while I was there, I used the opportunity to discover

Guadalajara, a city laid out much like cities of Europe. No surprise because it was designed by Napoleon's brother. There I discovered a street famous for its many Mariachi bands that lined along the roadway, all in different colored outfits. The specialty for these bands was to be hired to stand outside a window and serenade that very special person, sweetheart, or mother.

Traveling from there I visited a village on Lake Chapala where I fell in love with Mexican food, and visited the colorful markets where ladies made their special dishes, albondigas (herb meat balls), sopa de tortillas (tortilla soup), and tacos from a cart with roast beef, pork, or goat in a hot corn tortilla with a sprinkling of cilantro and salsa.

I liked the food and the area so much (and money seemed to go so far) I rented a villa with a front gateway so big you could enter on horseback and dismount. There was a plaza area with banana, lemon, and avocado trees, also flowers of all kinds. Beyond, looking out over the walls, was a view of Lake Chapala. The property had a twelve-foot wall, making the place private from nearby villas that had mixtures of animals. Dawn would be heralded with geese honking, ducks quacking, donkeys bellowing their he-haws, wild birds and parrots squawking—so much noise that you could only barely hear the roosters crowing.

I held on to this place almost until the coming salmon season. Because I still had almost a month before catching a flight to Alaska, and still had hopes of building my own boat, I went to Belize to check out prospects there where other Americans were building boats out of cement furrow, using local labor and exotic woods from nearby forests. I had heard about a man called German Joe who was building an all-wood boat in the jungle. He told me he had graduated from a nautical school in Europe and then worked on a sailing cruise ship for some time. He wanted to build his own ship, carving the shape out of wood. This spot had just what he needed—the wood and a river that overflows its banks each year. That would be the time of year to tow the hull to the coast for launching when he was finished.

He lived in a palapa hut on stilts six feet above the water at the time the river was over its banks. I was invited to stay and help him work, which I gladly did. The river was at its highest so we moved about the yard in a skiff with a long pole, alert for scorpions and water snakes. German Joe had a perfectly flat platform above water to lay out his bulkheads. A family of Mayan Indians harvested and delivered lumber for him for the two-masted ketch he was building. A ship that large could carry tons of cargo and with very high fuel prices, German Joe could do quite well by hauling goods between the islands in the Caribbean. I would have liked to see the project through to completion, but my visa was running out.

My return hit a snag because I didn't have papers for small-pox vaccination and was denied entry into Mexico. I went to a sort-of drugstore, a rather dirty place with few goods on the shelves. A lady from behind the counter got a syringe and vial from the refrigerator and I reluctantly allowed her to inject me with the vaccine. I really had no choice because without it I would not be allowed back into Quintana Roo, Mexico from where I would go to Lake Chapala, arrange for friends to stay in my villa for the summer of 1970, and once again return to Alaska in time for fishing season.

THROUGHOUT THAT SALMON season I couldn't stop thinking about building my own boat and continued mulling over various designs. I returned to the boat yard in Venice Beach, California and started looking at sailboats. Finally I bought plans for a forty-four-foot cutter, a beautiful craft that required only one person to sail it. It would be capable of going around the world. The boat yard in Venice Beach was no longer available so I ventured north to Ojai, near Oxnard, were I found a small one-bedroom house with one acre next to a main road. I thought I had everything in order but didn't realize I had been given an inappropriate and therefore invalid approval. So I kept working away and made great progress—right up until the moment city officials nailed up a stop work order and advised me I would need to put $2,500 in escrow in case I abandoned the project. That was the final straw so I dismantled the trestle I had built, sold or gave away the lumber, packed up my tools and headed for the San Francisco area where I knew several people from both college and Crested Butte.

For once, my timing couldn't have been better. I moved in with a friend from Crested Butte overlooking a grove of redwoods in Muir Woods National Monument. This was Marin County, just across the Golden Gate Bridge from San Francisco. The area was home to many rock bands and before long I found myself hanging out with musicians like Jerry Garcia of the Grateful Dead.

Somehow I survived my too-daring rides along the curvy Pacific Coast Highway with friends on a Norton 750 motorcycle and before I knew it, it was once again time to head for Kodiak.

During the 1971 salmon season, my shipmates and I lit up several celebratory cigars as we filled the hull with fish and had no more room to put any. When we headed for rendezvous with the tender ship, we would put up our feet and light yet another cigar, knowing the day's share for each of us would be about a thousand dollars.

Then it was back to Chapala in Mexico for just long enough to settle up with the landlord before heading to Ojo Caliente, a place in New Mexico I had been going to since my college days. The hot springs there have been continuously used for over a thousand years by Native Americans. When I first went there it was a dilapidated shack built over moss-covered rocks that surround the pool. The water was so hot the attendant had a strict twelve-minute limit on everyone. Once you were "cooked," he would lead you to a pallet and wrap you with an absorbent cotton blanket, then several layers of wool wrappings, until you looked like a mummy. The sweat poured out so profusely you could feel it. This treatment always left me so hungry I could hardly wait to get to a Mexican restaurant just across the highway where I could fill up on Mexican food and homemade sopapillas.

I always felt comfortable in New Mexico and was intrigued when I heard that an acquaintance had bought two hundred acres near La Madera for an incredible price. I started reading ads and looked at a few places until finally I found what I was looking for. It was one whole section of land, a 640-acre step back in time. It had a huge windmill with a 450-foot-deep well with cold clear water. An arroyo ran through the property with foothills of cedars, junipers and pinyon pines, fanning out onto the Plains of San Agustin.

Once again I was off on a new adventure. I was now a rancher.

I worked out a deal with owner financing, a down payment, and one payment every six months, buying a square mile of property with a house for a hundred and thirty-three dollars an acre. Built in the 1890s, the main building had a log room with a big fireplace; several additions had been made over three generations. The property was well fenced and sectioned off. There was a round breaking corral with a high fence and several other corrals made with fencing of cedar posts. There were three horse stalls and a building for hay storage, all made of logs. An old travel trailer served as a tack house for saddles and gear. On the other side of the house was a garage with a shop, built out of logs.

The tall windmill had a huge twelve-foot diameter fan to draw water to fill a 400-gallon tank for the house with an overflow filling a 7,000-gallon storage tank for stock and, in turn, that overflow filled a horse trough and eventually a half-acre pond I used to irrigate a one-acre garden.

Soon I had twenty-five steers, seven horses and a jackass, and from time to time I grazed a neighbor's cattle as well. Mostly I lived alone on a siesta schedule—awake before sun-up every day with a cup of coffee in hand as I sat on a stump and watched the sun rise over the mountains. I did any work that needed to be done early in the day, then had the biggest meal of the day around noon, usually something that I put on the wood-burning kitchen stove. After that I relaxed, maybe did some drawings, or worked on a scaled-down model of the cutter I almost built. Afternoons were often spent riding my horse Buster in the foothills, among the rock formations.

Morning sunrises were always spectacular. The sun lit the tops of the trees and moved down to light up the house then onto me, a nice moment until one day I saw a rattlesnake coiled up between my legs. That took my breath away and I was sure the snake could hear my heart pounding as I threw myself over backward and scrambled to my feet. From then on I had boots on when I had my morning coffee.

I spent a lot of time venturing into the vast, unoccupied and remote areas. I sometimes went off exploring for days and slept on the ground, surrounded by coyotes at night under a star-filled sky.

New Mexico is worthy of its motto—the Land of Enchantment. Its history reaches back long before the Spanish arrived in 1450 or thereabouts. Many structures were used long before the Spanish arrived, serving the same purposes a thousand years ago. My ranch was in an area so remote it was thirty-five miles to a one-room schoolhouse, and sixty miles to the nearest high school. Once or twice a month I drove about three hours for supplies either to El Paso or Albuquerque.

It was in El Paso that I met Delia, a student at UTEP (University of Texas at El Paso). Not long after I took the difficult step of selling the ranch I liked so much, I would see a lot of Delia, whom I came to call Dollie, as did everyone in her family. But then I was once again off to Alaska and another salmon season. That fall, Dollie transferred to the University of Texas in Austin so after the salmon season was over I headed straight for Austin and that is where Dollie and I began our lifelong relationship.

⁓

AFTER DOLLIE'S GRADUATION, we traveled to California, Colorado, New Mexico, and Missouri. Finally, we journeyed to the far western side of Michigan's upper peninsula. There we lived in the house that my grandfather built in 1911. It was in this same house that my father, aunts, and uncles had been born.

For Dollie and me skiing was a big draw in Michigan, with four ski areas within ten miles. Both Dollie and I worked for Indianhead Ski Area and we skied both alpine and cross country. I competed in the giant slalom events and heard the announcer refer to me as "the old man from Colorado, the oldest person in the event," even though I was only in my mid-thirties and wasn't from Colorado.

Canoeing was another favorite thing to do in the Upper Peninsula because you could get to places without a boat landing. There are so many lakes that you could portage from lake to lake, like in the Sylvania wilderness and also the Cisco chain of lakes that are connected by rivers and streams. Some rivers are canoe-able but as my cousin Ronny and I learned, some are not. On the Presque Isle, between US 2 and US 28, a distance of about 15 miles was more than expected. On that misadventure, Aunt Dorothy was to pick us up at US 28 at around 4 p.m. After it got dark my Aunt notified the Forest Ranger Station in Wakefield and told him two guys in a canoe were lost on the Presque Isle. We had known when we set out that we would have to portage around falls and rapids but way under-estimated all the tree falls and log jams. It was heavy going, hauling the canoe and gear over logs times beyond counting. Ron and I had different opinions on strategy, as he said we should head off into the woods and I insisted we stay on the river. I prevailed and finally we wearily trudged up onto the meeting place at midnight.

In 1981, my friend Bob Riley called with a new venture for me, just the kind I had never been able to resist. Let's reclaim silver, he proposed and described how we could recapture the precious metal from x-ray negatives. All I had to do was team up with him in Houston where he already had a place to work and one account in Beaumont. For sure with that account as a foundation, we would build a nice business from there. Made sense to me because the price of precious metals was skyrocketing and by a nice coincidence, Dollie's sister worked in the federal building in Houston. Soon we were off to the fast-growing city of Houston.

Dollie went back to school by enrolling at the University of Houston and I joined up with Bob, smelting silver from X-ray negatives and from the chemistry that they were developed in. We had that starter account with Methodist Hospital where they purged over a ton of X-ray negatives every six months. In time we added a number of clinics and chiropractic offices where we collected chemistry from their X-ray developers with hopes they would call us when purging film.

By law they had to keep X-rays for four years and then they could sell it for fifty percent of its estimated value in silver. We took the negatives to a refinery in Dallas where it was smelted for a percentage. Then we ran the chemistry through an electrolytic converter ourselves to get silver nitrate. It was no easy matter to make .999 silver until an old-timer taught us a trick that he said Incas used a thousand years earlier. After fluxing and pulling out all the impurities we could, we would plunge a branch from a willow tree into the molting metal and it would release that last bit of cadmium which left in a puff of smoke. A couple more steps and Presto! we were forming .999 pure bars in the shape of Texas.

An entirely new ingredient came into our lives on January 6, 1985 when Dollie delivered our son Paul. We moved into a bigger home in Katy, Texas and I quickly learned that being a father was the most exciting and rewarding role I had ever had.

⌐

Over the next several years, the price of silver continued to decline. Fortunately, Dollie now had her teaching certificate, and son Paul was almost ready for school. It was time for our son to get to know more of his family so it was back to Michigan once again.

We moved to Clinton Township, into a house built in the 1890s. The place had a huge barn, a three-car garage, and a shop, all on three acres with farm land that had not been farmed in more than twenty years. I immediately turned that ground into an organic farm with an acre and a half of vegetables I sold at a booth at the Royal Oak Farmers Market. The property also had apple and plum trees, raspberry bushes, and a grape vineyard. This is where we lived for the next twelve years while our son was going to elementary and junior high. The place was so natural that Paul's cub scout troop had campouts in our own secluded back yard, sheltered on the east and west by several rows of pine trees and by stands of maples on the north and catalpa trees along the road.

Aside from farming I worked for a time as an apprentice wood model maker. Dollie ran an English and Spanish translation business and taught Spanish to employees for companies in the area and then was hired into the Avondale School District to teach Spanish in high school.

I came across a new opportunity and bought into Country Grains Bread Company in Rochester. Now instead of mixing drinks at nights I was rolling dough—although not rolling *in* dough. But I did learn quickly from my business partner how to make great bread. The business had its good months but had too many slow periods because not enough people then were ready to pay four dollars for a loaf of bread. Even so, the early mornings sure smelled wonderful as the fresh bread cooled on the racks. My partner developed health issues and wanted me to buy him out. I delayed making a decision and when his patience ran out, he sold my equipment to Great Harvest and my time as a bread entrepreneur was toast.

IN 2001 WE moved to Sterling Heights so Paul could finish high school at nearby De La Salle before enrolling in the University of Michigan Engineering School. In 2007 we moved to a two-acre place in Independence Township. Dollie retired from teaching in 2015 and embarked on a career as a certified tour director leading groups of two dozen people to Cuba twice a month.

My quarter-acre vegetable garden yields a bounty of organic produce for our own consumption and that I also sell, along with eggs from my free-range chickens. I turn my hand once again to carving wood, making furniture, and drawing pictures.

For several years, the highlight of every week is Monday morning coffee at Brioni's in Clarkston with a group of like-minded folks. Their backgrounds vary considerably, as do the choices they have made along the way, but they share in common progressive values and offer stimulating perspectives on politics and current events. Every Monday morning session turns out to be as interesting and enjoyable as the things I have done in my life, from salmon fishing in Alaska to ranching in New Mexico to working the ski slopes of Colorado and Michigan, and even to managing a Playboy Club in Detroit. One exception only—being a partner to Dollie and a father. No occupation, no adventure could possibly top that.

5

BIG BEAVER – LIFE IN THE SLOW LANE
by Bill Haney

"... something really big was about
to happen in Big Beaver..."

FOR KIDS GROWING up in Big Beaver Village in the 1940s and
'50s, it felt as if their little hamlet was the one place on
Earth that time had passed by.

Many of them would say that was just hunky-dory.

To people motoring along Oakland County's countryside—
one mile road at a time—through the towns and cities along
Rochester Road, Big Beaver was barely worth slowing down
for. For folks from the north reaches of Oakland County, driving south toward Detroit from Clarkston, Rochester, Pontiac
and Waterford, the hamlet of Big Beaver came and went in
a minute or less. For cars headed northward from Clawson,
Royal Oak, Berkley, Ferndale and the bustling Motor City, the
most generous description of little Big Beaver was, with a pat
on the head, quaint.

No surprise that people thought of Big Beaver as a bit
threadbare, maybe even tacky. Just twenty years earlier, on
Rochester Road and a bit north of Maple Road, was the ram-

shackle Tent City. It had been set up by the government to house families that poured in from Ohio to Oklahoma with the men seeking work in the booming automobile plants. They found those jobs and before long saved up enough to get away from the squalor of Tent City. Climbing up the next rung on the socio-economic ladder, they built their own bare-subsistence living quarters. Many of them gouged out space in the farmland, clearing scrub acreage and the remaining orchards that once dominated the landscape. Some scraped up eighty dollars or so for a sixty-foot lot and slapped together a lean-to from scrap lumber over a dirt floor or erected a makeshift house from cinder blocks. As jobs steadied and wages increased, they took another step up and built modest frame homes.

Despite its awkward growing pains, Big Beaver wasn't without its charms, some notable commercial operations, and even a few tourist attractions. There were roadside stands offering apples and peaches, fresh vegetables, fresh-slaughtered beef and pork, chickens, turkeys, and eggs. Weekend evenings featured country hoe-downs at May's Barn Dance with carloads of regulars from the area joining in to square dance and dance the polka with local folk. Too soon for the youngsters, the strains of *Goodnight, Sweetheart* would signal closing time, with teenage boys wishing they could croon like Bing Crosby, hoping the moonlight and the soft summer breeze on the walk home would bring a goodnight kiss:

> *Goodnight sweetheart, 'til we meet tomorrow*
> *Goodnight sweetheart, sleep will banish sorrow*
> *Tears and parting may make us forlorn*
> *But with the dawn a new day is born*
> *So I'll say goodnight sweetheart,*
> *though I'm not beside you*

Goodnight sweetheart, still my love will guide you
Dreams enfold you and in each one I'll hold you
Goodnight sweetheart, goodnight

～

JUST UP ROCHESTER Road two miles and west two miles almost to Crooks Road, stood gleaming White Chapel Mausoleum and its sedate cemetery and somber monuments to those who died in war. On Rochester Road north of Long Lake Road was the most popular attraction in all of Oakland County, the Salt Water Swimming Pool, drawing throngs from miles around. The boastful sign at Long Lake Road said it all— "Saltier than the Great Salt Lake."

Not least, Big Beaver was well situated in the middle of Troy Township, smack between Royal Oak and Rochester, and next door to Birmingham and Bloomfield Hills. If someday those cities grew too crowded or expensive, little Big Beaver with all those farms and vacant land might benefit from the overflow and become an actual city itself. As if that would ever happen, we school kids scoffed. They'd probably give it a dumb name like Troy, or something.

Heading north into the lakes area, the intersection of Big Beaver Road and Rochester Road was the last place you could buy gasoline until you got to the town of Rochester which was another seven miles to the north and no sure thing in an old jalopy. So if you were running on fumes while headed to the Salt Water Swimming Pool or to the lakes, you might better mind your fuel gauge. Best to fill up at Haney's Oil Well Sunoco Gasoline and Service Station while you had the chance.

There was more. If you had a few minutes and an interest in local lore, you might catch a good story at the Oil Well. It was presided over by my father, Raymond (Red) Haney, ex--marine, boxer, vehicle mechanic, and spinner of tales told so convincingly that some endure, accepted as fact to this day. One such is the yarn about how the very name Big Beaver was coined, a whimsical fable indeed, too long for these pages, but retold in my book, *From Big Beaver to the Big Apple.*

That main intersection was also the village's heart of commerce. On the southeast corner was Miller & Lorre's Tavern, a local landmark destined to morph into one bar after another—Doc's "It" Club, The Wagon Wheel, and finally, Hooters. A hundred yards to the east was C.F. Long Towing & Salvage where you went for yet-another transmission for your '38 Plymouth or rummaged among the hulks for a matching fender. You could find whatever steering wheel knob or fancy hood ornament you wanted for fifty cents apiece or "take the whole bushel basketful and gimme five dollars." Farther east almost to John R there was Main Airport, just opened in 1946. There, Cessnas and Piper Cubs would practice takeoffs and landings all day long, a sight that never got old for preteen boys watching from their Roadmaster or Schwinn bikes.

Just south of Big Beaver Road, on the east side of Rochester Road was the sometimes hardware store next door to Beaver Feed & Grain, proprietor Wesley Smith, the mecca for the many families who raised various fowl and small animals, as well as larger livestock.

On the northwest corner of Rochester and Big Beaver Roads, a trio of businesses—Kleitch's Meat Market & Grocery, the Home Bakery, and Haney's Oil Well. Just a few yards to the north, on the site of the long since abandoned one-room school, the Troy Honor Roll, stood tall and proud. On that gleaming, white-painted billboard were the names of six hundred twenty-three of the eight hundred twenty-six men and women from Troy Township who served in the military during World War II. The entire Township had fewer than four thousand citizens and nearly one-quarter of them were in military service.

Red Haney had spearheaded the creation of the Honor Roll and that, of course, meant he volunteered me to maintain the stubborn patch of grass in front of the big billboard. Until my prayers were answered and the hot summer sun parched the scraggly grass into dormancy, I spent many hours fighting a losing battle with a rusty mower that gummed up a dozen blades for every one it cut.

Right across Rochester Road on the east side was a tiny forerunner to the modern-day strip mall. There were three store fronts, including at various times the Adams and Ogg barber shops, a mini-pool hall, soda bars, and the offices of Dr. Donald Reid, the only medical man within miles. In the middle unit, a Kroger grocery store gave way after the War to a succession of drug stores and soda bars with names like Fitzgerald's, DiFabio's and eventually, Gill's. I worked there on and off when it was Fitzgerald's pharmacy/soda bar/liquor store, putting up stock and sweeping and polishing floors for fifty cents an hour, glad to get it.

One evening I found myself thrust into emergency service jerking sodas, not the first time I was conscripted into a job I knew nothing about. I had gone back into the storeroom for a jar of raspberry syrup for a banana split I was making. There I found all three of my bosses—the mother, father, and son who owned the place. Two were collapsed onto the couch, one sprawled on the floor, all three drunk out of their skulls.

One rainy night I was over-loaded with work as my three bosses were yet again heavily lubricated in the back room. All day long customers had tracked in mud, so after I closed for the night, I engaged Gerry Moore to help me mop and wax the floor. He stopped half way through a swipe and said, "Hey, I just created another invention."

Gerry was always creating inventions.

"What it is," Gerry announced, "is a wax that is as shiny

after it dries as it is when it is wet."

I thought about it. "Good one, Gerry. But how do you make it shiny like that?"

"Hey, I invent them. Somebody else's job to make the stuff."

And he resumed sloshing on the wax you could see your reflection in now but that would be dull when it dried, not like the stuff he had just invented.

One short block to the north, Lovell's Fruit Stand had done so well they enlarged it into a mini-regular grocery store. Not a hundred feet across Meadowcrest Street was Vern Bauer's Market, right alongside his sister's place, Robinson's Soda Bar. And barely a quarter mile north, T.J. Torpey opened up a butcher shop and Joe Nephew enlarged his fruit stand into yet another grocery store. One season I worked for Mr. Nephew and was taught his one edict: "When telling a customer a price, the word is 'dollar,' not 'buck.' We never say, 'That'll be a buck and a half.' No, we say, 'That will be a dollar and fifty cents, sir or ma'am'." Okay. I'll try to remember that, sir. Or ma'am.

In the summers, just up the road a piece, at 16 and 1/2 Mile Road, was Cobb's Corn Stand, a name too perfect to be a coincidence. The kindly old couple sold corn so sweet your teeth would ache just thinking about it. Full-size ears went for a quarter a baker's dozen. A baker's dozen might be thirteen ears, maybe fifteen or sixteen. We seldom got full-sized because Mrs. Cobb would usually give me a big smile and a bigger bag to fill. She would say, "If you're willing to pick 'em your own self, you just bag all the nubbins you want. Shuck 'em on the spot. Nickel the dozen, two bits all you can fit into this here bag."

The nubbins were Golden Bantam ears that never reached full size but made up for it in crisp sweetness. I would trudge out into the field where Mr. Cobb would be harvesting. He would say, "Hope your mom has the water to boiling. You know the saying—if you trip on the way home and spill 'em on the ground, you gotta go back for fresh. Billy, you know why?" I did know why, I always knew why, but he never gave me a chance. "I'll tell you why—'cause then the sugar's already turning to starch and they're only fit to feed to the hogs."

Lest you've lost count, that makes five grocery stores, a soda bar or two, a butcher shop, a kind of hardware store, one salvage yard purveying previously owned car parts, a couple summer vegetable stands, the feed and grain store, two barber shops, a tavern, and one gas station in well less than half a mile. There was also the Methodist Church, right alongside May's Barn Dance. Was that a metropolis, or what?

Five miles to the north was the biggest agricultural spread around, operated by Ferry-Morse, the world's largest seed company. My three older brothers had worked there in the 1930s, as did many Big Beaver boys. They would trudge along behind trailers towed by muscular Clydesdales or massive "one-lung" tractors. The boys' job was to pick up and toss onto the trailers those cantaloupes, green peppers, and tomatoes that had fallen off on the way in for processing into next year's dime seed packets. But not all vegetables made it all the way to the processing plant in those deep Depression days. Some would get damaged by sheer accident and left on the ground to be gathered up once it was dark, after which they would magically appear on Big Beaver's dinner tables.

Eventually, at one time or another, one task or another, I would work at several of those places. A few jobs paid a quarter or so an hour; some places paid in barter, with whatever they had on hand.

For chores around the house, Mom handed me a quarter a week along with a dose of conscience, "I know you want to do your part to help feed the poor in Africa. You know, Billy, they aren't as well off as we are. Wouldn't it feel good to put a dime for them in Sunday's collection envelope?"

Well, Mom, actually, no. But after having had that quarter all of two minutes, I'd fork it over and get a nickel and a dime back, if I was lucky. Not so easy come, but very easy go.

Parents had no end of lines like that. When I hadn't cleaned my plate, it was, "Somebody hasn't finished their nice squash. What wouldn't the starving children in India do for that?" No explanation for how my slab of squash tasty as a hockey puck would make its way onto a plate in Bombay.

Praying and sacrificing and church were a big part of life during those World War years, from 1942 to '45. Especially for my mother, who in 1918 had converted from Protestantism to marry my Irish Catholic father. Perhaps she had become all the more devout during the war years when she had three sons and a son-in-law in combat. I was doing my part, kneeling next to my mother even before the sun came up every morning. We would say one rosary, one novena, one Stations of the Cross after another and still we would go off to church more than seemed necessary to cleanse the soul of a growing boy.

Mom, a fine pianist, was also the organist at Guardian Angles Church in Clawson where the few Roman Catholic families in Big Beaver were parishioners. My sister and I sat alongside mother in the tiny organist's balcony and sang hymns and responses in Latin to the priest in high mass. But even that wasn't enough, so we would duck into the little church when in the vicinity to pray for any and all in combat and for that boy with the big goiter in his neck because he didn't get enough iodine from not eating his codfish. He could have mine.

People got involved in whatever patriotic ways they could. Few were the houses without an American flag waving from a pole jammed into a standout bracket by the front porch door. Most of the homes also had a banner hanging prominently in a front window with one or more blue stars on it. Those banners proudly proclaimed how many family members were in military service.

My mother was president of the Blue Star Mothers, maybe because we had two sons in the Marines, one in the Air Force, and a son-in-law in the Navy. So mother hosted meetings at our house to knit items for service men or to wrap packages for overseas shipment.

One day I walked past a house on Boyd Street just at the moment Mrs. Ogg took down her banner with its blue star. She replaced it with a new banner. This one had a gold star. She saw me watching and went quickly back into the house without so much as a smile. When I got home, I asked my Mother why couldn't we have a gold star like the Oggs. Her face fell and she said, "Oh, Billy, don't ever say such a thing." She couldn't talk for a while. Later on she took me aside and we sat on the piano bench while she explained that a gold star meant a son, or a husband, or some relative had been killed in military action.

All the Blue Star Mothers and most other families rendered out fat from bacon—and beef, when they could get it—and poured the drippings into cans. There the bacon fat would congeal and that meant it wouldn't make a mess when somehow it was magically turned into something useful for the war. How do they do that—make a bullet out of bacon fat? What're they going to think of next?

It was easier to understand ration books. I heard on the radio that there was only so much rubber, gasoline, metal, and sugar in the world and if it was wasted, the Germans and Japanese would win. So everyone had their own ration book and pages of special little stamps to tear off for rationed items.

In addition to Mother's "legitimate" roles at church, she also became the central figure in a scandal. Catholic churches were well known for their fund-raising events—raffles, rummage sales, minstrel shows, white elephant sales, and bazaars. Once every year, my Mother dressed as a gypsy and told fortunes, reading tea leaves and palms. She had her hair all done up with a scarf and sparkling barrettes and had lots of makeup and big shiny earrings. After the 1944 bazaar, the parish priest called her into his office and spoke quietly with her, while they had me sit outside in the hallway.

When she came out, Mother's face was ashen and her hands trembled. Only later did I learn that the priest had told her he regretted she would no longer be able to tell fortunes at the bazaars. Several upset parishioners had come forward to say that everything that the "Gypsy Madeline Haney" had foretold had come true. Because the Church officially banned witchcraft and fortune-telling, there was no way to explain how her predictions had been so accurate.

When I asked Mother about it, she shook her head and said, "I can't explain it either. I was just telling the person what I saw."

In those war years, one way or another, nearly everyone did their part. Women staffed the Red Cross and various auxiliaries. They were always going to meetings or gathering for work Bees. Men were involved in Civil Defense and night-time patrols. Those who were too old or otherwise not qualified to be in military service worked extra jobs, often in plants making airplanes, tanks, other vehicles, and products needed by the military. It seemed that everyone in Michigan was proud that Detroit was "the Arsenal of Democracy."

Daytime jobs weren't enough for most people. Parents taught children how to tell a vegetable plant from a weed so they could tend the family's "Victory Garden." Evenings or Saturdays, a small cluster of men would pile into a flatbed truck. Off key but with plenty of volume, they would sing *The Caissons Go Rollin' Along; Anchors Aweigh; Nothing Can Stop the Army Air Corps; The Marine's Hymn;* and *Over There* as they bounced along on the gravel roads. They scoured neighborhoods south to Clawson and north towards Rochester Village, searching for metal treasures. Unless someone had already picked a place clean, they would find prime pickings at the small farms along Wattles Road and Long Lake Road from Dequindre to Adams Roads, rummaging through barns and scavenging behind garages and tool sheds to unearth usable metal.

Because most able-bodied men were off to war, women stepped up and stepped into roles previously closed to them. My oldest sister, Madeline, was among the local versions of the popular poster girl "Rosie, the Riveter." She gave up her job as a telephone operator to help assemble B-24 "Liberator" bombers at Ford's Willow Run plant. That was the same type of aircraft my brother Dick flew for several dozen missions over Germany and Eastern Europe. We often wondered if Madeline had worked on an airplane brother Dick flew.

Youngsters were not exempt and they didn't want to be because almost every boy or girl had someone near and dear to them in uniform. Teachers assigned students to write letters during class time to servicemen. Kids wanted to be able to report to their overseas father, brother, or uncle that they too were doing their part. Teachers also administered War Bond Drives.

I had heard jingles on the radio and had seen posters with Uncle Sam pointing a bony finger at me, ordering me to buy War Bonds. Teachers said the way it worked was to buy special stamps for a quarter apiece. If I did that every week, in just ten years from when I started pasting those stamps into my booklet, I would get back almost three cents extra for every dollar I put in. I couldn't believe that the government would actually give me free money like that, just for holding on to mine for ten years. At the same time, I was helping win the War.

I looked forward to that very special day when I would be able to paste the very last stamp into my booklet. By then I would be a senior in high school in 1954 and could cash it in and collect all the money I had earned. That would help pay for my college education. What a country.

⁓

I LEARNED LOTS of lessons during the War. For one thing, even a little kid could sometimes be useful. Who would have have thought that? There was more to life, my father told me more than once, than just "fooling around wasting time or sleeping in the sun." I don't recall ever having slept in the sun. Well, I suppose I might have fooled around and wasted time once in a while.

In 1946, after my brothers had come home from the War, brothers Dick and Bob let me caddie for them. That got me started with something I would do in the summers for the next several years. But that was only a few months a year. Once summer was over, I wouldn't be wading the creeks for golf balls and caddying once in a while at Sylvan Glen.

One morning I was out watching Floyd "Mike" Rankin, our janitor at Big Beaver School, run the American flag up the flag pole. We lived only about fifty steps from the school, so sometimes I would be over there bouncing a ball against the wall when Mike did the flag. He asked me if I ever did anything but bounce that ball. I told him, "Sure." I was glad he didn't ask me for details.

Then he asked , "Don't you know that an idle hand is the devil's workshop?" I had to think how to answer that, even though my father has said it so many times I wanted to roll my eyes until all you could see was the whites. But instead I told Mike that was why I was looking for a job so what did he think of that. He kind of snorted and said if I knew how to push a broom and work a dust rag, we might could work something out.

The next day I started the job I would have for the next four years. When school was in session, my work began right after final bell. I would be making twenty-five cents an hour, paid every Friday evening, when—as became our routine—we'd have a hamburger, fries and a double chocolate malt at Robinson's Soda Bar. When I paid Mrs. Robinson, I also thought, Well, there went three hours work. But it was like Mike and I were celebrating that we'd made it through another week.

One evening, just out of the blue, Mike pulled his bony frame up like he was standing at attention. He put on a serious face and said, "You see before you the chief custodial engineer for Big Beaver Schools."

I asked Mike if that made me assistant chief custodial engineer. He said he guessed maybe it did just so long as I didn't ask for a raise just because I now had a fancy title.

When I was in class, I didn't talk with the other kids about my job and title—I acted like I was just a regular school kid like them, even though I was now a member of the labor force. During those school hours, my own classroom was in the old brick building that Mike told me had been built around 1900. It was attached by a passageway to what we called the "new school," a two-story brick building built in 1925 for junior high and high school. One great thing about the school was that it had bathrooms and that was a big step up from the house I lived in and its outdoor privy.

In 1947, when I was in my second year as Mike's helper, he told me I would now be earning thirty-five cents an hour and asked what I thought of that. I said let's go over to Robinson's Soda Bar and I'll treat.

The war had been over for two years. Rationing was a thing of the past. All kinds of products were available again. When new cars came out, boys argued over who would be the first to see the newest models. Special housing for veterans had been built at Willow Run by the government and one of my brothers and a sister and their new babies lived there in small box-like places for twenty-eight dollars a month. I no longer had to do my own tour of duty atop old Tede Dungereaux's ash pile. All during the war I had been a sentry. It wasn't something I had been ordered to do. I just kind of knew it had to be done, so I volunteered, not telling anyone but just standing guard with my Red Ryder BB gun cocked and ready in case the Japanese or German troops came sweeping over the North Pole to invade Big Beaver. I had seen plenty of war movies and knew you just couldn't be too sure. So, every once in a while I'd clamber up there, atop Tede's ash pile, to keep an eye out to the north, just in case the Russians got any funny ideas.

In those postwar days, that geographic dot we knew as Big Beaver was far too small to show up on almost any map. Some adults seemed embarrassed to say they lived in Big Beaver, so they would say Troy Township, or maybe just, "I live out in the country, north of Detroit." But mail delivered to our house had the address as Rural Route #1, Birmingham. It could get confusing.

When we went shopping, we would take the Martin Bus Line south to Royal Oak or north to Rochester, drop a nickel in the fare box. On special occasions, like Christmas shopping, we would go to the huge Federal's department store in Pontiac. Some kids told me their parents took them shopping all the way down to J.L. Hudson's in Detroit. They even went to the big Thanksgiving Day Parade down Woodward Avenue. Or so they said.

My parents never did that and I'd just as soon my friends didn't talk about how swell it was. And how they stopped at Sanders in Royal Oak on the way home and got to order whatever they wanted, which was always a thirty-five cent cream-puff hot fudge sundae, another thing I only heard plenty of but never saw, let alone got to order. If you asked me, they made it all up. I did get to go to Saturday matinees at the five movie theaters in Royal Oak, Clawson and Rochester, and roller skating at Ambassador Roller Skating Rink in Clawson, so that was something.

I thought about those things while I was sweeping the floor in the school library, my most special place in all of Big Beaver School. It was even more special than the high school study hall that was really two regular rooms with a sliding door in between so you could open it up for Friday night sock hops after football games. That was when the Blue Notes Combo played and with the windows opened I could hear the Ernst brothers electric guitar all the way over to my house. When Ed "Sonny" Herweyer belted out *That Lucky Old Sun*, just like Frankie Laine, the girls wanted to swoon.

I knew our tiny library wasn't like the fancy ones they must have in Birmingham or Bloomfield Hills but I couldn't imagine anything better than being able to take a book off a shelf and have it be like your very own for two weeks. I usually finished a book the same day or maybe two, but I would read the good ones twice. "Trying to see if it will come out the same way the second time?" Miss Earla Smith, the English teacher who also ran the library, would always say that. I always pretended it was the first time and laughed anyhow because I knew she meant it in a good way.

The library was so small I could sweep the floor one pass up and one pass back. It was squeezed in there on the second floor of the high school, next to the principal's office and the girl's bathroom—which I also had to clean, but that's another story. It once had been what we called a cloak room, fancy name for a long, skinny closet. But now that the war was over, all kinds of things—like typewriters—could be built again. So most folks—except really old guys like my father—had gotten used to women working and that meant that high school girls were training to be secretaries.

The bad thing was that by the time I was in junior high, my wonderful library was gone. I had been turned into a junky, cramped typing classroom. Not only were all the books gone, now it was messier to clean because half the time the girls just dropped their gum on the floor instead of sticking it onto the underside of a desk like civilized people do, so now I had to get a putty knife and scrape it up before it hardened right into the wood floor.

My duties were the same most every day after final bell and the kids were gone for the day. Wipe the blackboards. Soak up the chalk dust on the blackboard tray on a dampened cloth. Empty the wastepaper baskets and get a whiff of that mixture of apple cores, orange peels, and pencil sharpenings. Then I would flick out a couple handfuls of my sweeping compound to keep down the dust while I swept up the dirt tracked in on muddy galoshes. Once the dust has settled, wipe down the desks with a cloth with oil sprinkled on it. There's a right way and a wrong way to do everything.

While I worked, I would practice singing the jingles I heard on the radio, or mimic the wise cracks that the high school kids said:

— *"You're cruisin' for a bruisin' and ridin' for a fall"*
— *"Pepsi Cola hits the spot, twelve full ounces, that's a lot..."*
— *"That's for me to know and for you to find out"*
— *"I'm Chiquita Banana and I come to say, bananas gotta ripen in a certain way..."*
— *"Don't paint the devil on the wall"* (It took me a while to figure out that meant stop talking about all the bad things that might happen or they might come true.)
— *"You're not even dry behind the ears"* (Every time an adult said that to me I felt like saying, Yeah, and I bet the back of your ears have been dry for about two centuries. But I knew that would get me my own ears boxed.)
— *"He's got the gift of gab"*
— *"I'm all at 6's and 7's"* (I guessed that meant you were so flustered you couldn't make up your mind.)

Or I would just practice my spelling or memorize poems—anything not to be wasting time while I was doing my rounds. But sometimes during those nice warm spring afternoons, I would hear from out the open window the sounds of a ball getting whacked by a bat. Then I would speed up so I could get out while there was still time before kids would get called in for supper. Mike Rankin kind of knew that so he'd let me off without extra jobs those evenings.

Then I'd hurry out to the ball field behind the school and get into a good left-field-only game with Jerry Wyett, Junior and Chuckie Gardner, Bobby Adams and whatever kids might show up. Sometimes they would grumble that I had messed up the ball field with the four-hole golf course I had built on it.

But they knew my golf course really didn't bother the baseball playing all that much. Besides, those guys played on my golf course just as much as I did, whacking the cut-up balls with two broken clubs my brother Dick gave me. Before the baseball game started, we would take the little flagpoles out of the cups I had made out of Del Monte peaches cans, so the only problem was if you were running for a fly ball and happened to step in a cup. That only happened a few times.

Every once in a while, my Dad would show up at one of our pick-up games with a big box. When he opened it, it was like a cloud of steam except that it was a cold puff that would rise up from the slabs of dry ice that kept the ice cream frigid. Dad would say the Frost-Bites and Dairy Cups were "just day-old stuff" from work—he meant from H.A. McDonald's Creamery where he was the mechanic for the delivery trucks. Most of the left-overs he would take to the nuns in the convent next to the creamery, but this time there was plenty of day-old stuff. Didn't taste day-old to us.

My father was a real snob about genuine dairy products. For one thing, he wouldn't have margarine in the house. I remember often having dinner those days at Jerry Wyett's house. I loved Mrs. Wyett's chipped beef and Jolly Green Giant frozen peas over white sauce on toast with butter melting on top. But sometimes when butter couldn't be had, I would watch Mrs. Wyett do her magic on a pound of margarine. She would let the margarine warm up enough and then hand it to me to squish around until a little bubble of yellow-orange coloring liquid in the bag would break. Then you could work that glob of orange-ish dye into the white clump of margarine and before you knew it, you had made instant butter. Kind of. When I told my dad about this marvelous stuff, he just snorted and shook his head.

⟿

THERE WASN'T MUCH to do in February 1950 because it was so cold your tongue would freeze on the flagpole when you went to lick the frost off, something you weren't likely to do a second time. Once was sure enough for me. The snow wouldn't pack and there was no smooth ice for pond hockey. I had read all the books and gone through Jack Todd's great stack of comic books twice but that was okay because now we had our very own television set.

For a couple years my father had been saying, "I'll never have a television set in this house. Waste of time and money. Three channels and not a thing worth watching." Then he heard they were going to televise *Gillette's Friday Night Fights*. That meant that Red Haney, a one-time boxer and trainer, could for the first time see the greats: Willie Pep, Sugar Ray Robinson (the original one), and Jake LaMotta. The next day, at a time when my frugal father was making less than one hundred dollars a week, he came home with a four-hundred dollar Emerson ten-inch black and white set.

Every now and then we got a good picture—as long as you cocked the rabbit ears antenna just right and had your eyeballs less than maybe seven feet away. That was okay because the first few months I would just sit on the floor and watch the test pattern until the serials and cartoons came on. In the evenings, I was assigned to hold one arm of the rabbit ears while lifting my left leg just so, until my sister said, "Hold it right there. Okay, now bark."

I told my sister she was a real wit—or at least half that.

One day I experimented. I ran a wire from the rabbit ears to a metal curtain rod and Presto! a sharp picture. If my sister had come up with that idea, my Dad would have said she should be on Mt. Rushmore. Since I dreamed it up, it was like,

"So? What've you done for me lately." But I didn't care because now I could lie on the floor and watch *The Lone Ranger* and my other shows and college football and basketball on weekends. The biggest treat was the third period of Detroit Red Wings games—the only period then televised. The fuzzy picture seemed to never sharpen up and the horizontal hold was always going out. Only years later did I learn that those hockey games were played using a puck.

But for all the entertaining sports and serials and variety shows like *Ed Sullivan, Milton Berle,* and *Sid Caesar*, the most compelling television in early 1950 was something else. One teacher called it, "History happening before our very eyes."

I knew something important was happening when Senator Joseph McCarthy shook a fist, waved a stack of papers, and shouted. He said he had the names of more than two hundred people who were card-carrying Communists working in government jobs and in universities. He said they were plotting to overthrow the United States government and take over the country.

One day I was in Mr. Jim Adams barber shop, listening to three men sitting around the big pot-belly stove as they argued about McCarthy. One man said Senator McCarthy really knew about these things. He said he was standing up for patriotic Americans against the threat of the "Red menace that is about to wash over our shores and make it illegal to go to church and believe in God." Another man said no, McCarthy never showed any evidence for what he was claiming, and until he did, it was just a witch hunt to get publicity and get his face on television.

My English teacher, Miss Earla Smith, said, "Some things you just have to pay careful attention to and make up your own mind about." Lot of help that was.

‑‑

I HAD SPENT most of the years during and after the war finding ways I could make a little bit more money for myself as well as to please my mother by helping those starving children in Africa and India. Lots of my jobs depended on the weather and whether school was in session. They included hunting for golf balls at Sylvan Glen Golf Course and caddying at Red Run Golf Club; picking strawberries and cherries; mowing lawns; and substituting for the *Pontiac Press* or *Detroit Times* delivery boys. Or whatever came along, like helping out at the local grocery stores; setting pins at Clawson Bowling Lanes for a nickel a line; and most steadily, helping Mike the janitor.

Most jobs I had to go look for. One sunny August morning in 1949, a job came to me.

I was hitchhiking to Detroit to see the Tigers play at Briggs Stadium. A big dark blue Cadillac stopped and the driver, a fancy-dressed woman, asked me where I was going. I told her and she motioned for me to get in. After scolding me for hitch-hiking and asking me lots of questions, she asked if I was "a boy who knows what work is." I told her the jobs I had done—janitor's assistant at Big Beaver Schools, caddying, and picking berries, and... "Quite enough," she said, "But if your busy schedule permitted, do you like to climb trees?" That was an easy one, and so then she asked would I like a job helping out her husband in his little apple orchard. She handed me a small card that said she was Dr. Harrington. A woman doctor. What's next? She told me her husband was retired now but had been a catcher in the Tigers' minor leagues before his knee gave out.

If I was really serious about working, I should call him to discuss details and talk about pay. She thought he might go as high as fifty cents an hour for a good worker who minded his

P's & Q's and didn't give sass.

It was a smooth ride along Woodward in her nice car into downtown Detroit. She pointed to a building and said that was where she had her office. But then she drove right past it and took me right to the corner of Michigan and Trumbull. I got there so early I saw batting practice.

The next morning, I called and talked to Mr. Harrington and got directions. I got off the Martin bus right in front of his house, just south of Leader Dogs for the Blind, near the corner of Avon and Rochester Roads. He showed me around the place and told me what my jobs would be. He said he'd call me in the fall when the apples were ripe and ready for picking.

～

TWO MONTHS LATER, early one Saturday morning, he set me to work gleaning the windfalls in the soft grass under the trees. Mr. Harrington stood off to the side and watched me the whole time. He said the windfalls were good for cider, as long as they didn't show signs of worms or bruising. The apples to be sold by the bag were for eating out of hand and for pies, and those wanted to be picked off the trees. Then he set up a long ladder and had me climb the trees for everything I could reach. When he went inside the house for something, I got off the ladder and crept out onto the limbs where the picking was better.

I had several crates full, with the culls separated from the keepers, when Mr. Harrington returned. I could smell something and saw that he had opened up what turned out to be his first pint for the day of Old Overholt rye whiskey.

He lit up a cigarette and watched as I moved the bagged apples off to the side and then loaded the cider-apple crates into the trailer he had hitched up to his car. Mr. Harrington motioned toward the car so I got into the passenger side of his brand-new Cadillac Sedan de Ville, the same as Dr. Harrington's except for the tan color. But then he got in on my side and kind of pushed me over onto the driver's side.

"Here," he said, and handed me the keys. "You drive. I need to rest my eyes."

He didn't ask if I had a driver's license or even if I knew how to drive, and by the time I thought maybe I had better tell him, he was snoring. I had learned long ago it was not a good idea to wake a sleeping adult.

For years, I had watched my parents drive our stick-shift Fords. "Damned if I'll pay a hundred eighty-five dollars to have somebody shift for me," Dad said. Lawrence Smith was only fourteen years old and he had been driving truck forever, it seemed. I had driven bumper cars at Bob-Lo so I guessed that a regular car must not be anything special. Just bigger. So what's the big deal, driving a Cadillac?

One thing I noticed, Mr. Harrington's de Ville didn't have a clutch pedal. It took me a while to figure things out, but he was sound asleep and we didn't seem to be on a tight schedule. Pretty soon I got the car started and worked the shift lever until we were moving. I got a lot of practice going forward and back, what with towing that trailer that had its own way of doing things. But before long we were straightened away and heading out the driveway. By sitting way forward on the seat, I could reach the brake and gas pedals and that way I could see through the windshield by looking under the top of the steering wheel and just over the dashboard.

I didn't even have to go out onto Rochester Road because I saw that I could drive on the gravel shoulder the short way up to Avon Road. There I had to turn right to get to Yates Cider Mill, where I had been a few times with my folks.

Mr. Harrington woke up when I stopped kind of abruptly after I pulled into the cider mill parking lot. He put down the window and pointed to a long conveyor belt running into the mill and waved for me to drive over there. I did that and then he made hand signs for me to empty the apples onto the belt, and hit the big red button he pointed at. I dumped the apples like he said and walked alongside as the apples rolled smoothly on the conveyor belt, making sure all of them made it on right into the mill.

There were no lights on in the dark mill house and the only sound was the machinery just running on its own. I called out but there was nobody in the entire place. Soon all the apples were gone from the belt and down into a big bin. All of a sudden, there were all kinds of noises as the big press started up. I looked around to see who was controlling all this, but there was not a single person in the place and Mr. Harrington was still out there in his car. It was like everything was happening by magic. In a few minutes, spigots were pouring fresh cider into gallon jugs that turned and stopped on a turntable as the cider poured into each jug, stopping within an inch of being full.

"Here, put these on," Mr. Harrington said, coming up from behind and startling me. He handed me a small cardboard box half full of bottle caps printed with "Harrington's Fresh Apple Cider."

Driving back, I had to be even more careful because I had to turn left twice, at the intersection of Avon and Rochester Roads, and then again into Harrington's driveway. Good thing Mr. Harrington was sound asleep again when I made that last left turn into his driveway; he was snoring so loudly he didn't even wake up despite all those horns blowing.

After I parked the car, I just sat there for a while and thought about it.

Finally I got out and looked around for what to do next. Alongside the front porch, I found a big white sign with "Apples & Cider - For Sale" on each side. I stood it up in the gravel near the road where you could see it from either direction. By the time I had unloaded the bottles of cider and carried the peck and half-peck bags of choice apples to the picnic table on the front porch, our first customer had parked in the gravel and was walking across the lawn. My first sale. If only I knew what I was supposed to charge. Mr. Harrington would know but he was sleeping so comfortably in his car I didn't want to disturb him.

In another three weeks, my apple orchard job was over for the season.

⌒

THE NEXT YEAR, Dr. Harrington called and invited me back, but a lot had changed. I had gotten my first step up the ladder in golf from being a caddie. I was in charge of the caddie shack at Red Run Golf Club in Royal Oak, making nearly sixty cents an hour for ten hours a day, six days a week and free golf on Mondays, all summer long and weekends in the fall. I had a real title instead of a caddie badge: I was the assistant to the assistant caddie master at one of Michigan's historic country clubs. Here I was, fourteen years old with a title and a position in management.

Not only did I have a job, something really big was about to happen in Big Beaver. In just another year a big new Class B school at Livernois and Big Beaver Road would be open. There were going to name it Troy High School.

The talk was it would have all kinds of stuff we had never had before. Best of all, we'd have our very own gymnasium and a basketball court so we didn't have to play every game on the road. Our two Class D schools—Big Beaver and Log Cabin—would be put together with the half dozen elementary schools in Troy Township and from now on all the kids from miles around would be going to Troy High. Not only would we have football, baseball, and basketball, there would be golf and track, and girl's sports. There would be band, glee club, speech, and debate. For kids who had grown up in schools with only the bare necessities, it was hard to believe this was really going to happen.

It seemed that life just couldn't get any better. I thought about how different it was going to be around these parts. I also began to realize something else—the Big Beaver where I was born and had lived my entire life would never be the same again.

6

DEN'S EXCELLENT MILITARY ADVENTURE
by Dennis Ritter

"Our new mother then told us that we were to march to an empty barracks to drop off our bags and relax before the G.I. Party was to begin. Everyone looked at each other and was excited—we're having a party. A Welcome-to-the-Army party. Was this gonna be a fun place or what!"

IN THE 1930s and '40s, *Cheaper by the Dozen* was a popular book and Hollywood movie. I don't know if that gave my parents any ideas but when I was born on August 28, 1945, I was the eighth child of Kevin J. and Mary E. Ritter of Pontiac, Michigan. My arrival took my parents two-thirds of the way to what would be the Ritter dozen, with seven boys and five girls.

My baptism was delayed, however, until both my godparents, Uncle John and Aunt Annette Carry could do the honors. So, that happened after Uncle John returned safely from Europe in WWII.

We lived in a very large house that had six bedrooms with two full bathrooms at 73 Auburn Avenue and Parke Street—

what is now Wide Track Drive. The house was purchased from the daughter of Hazen Pingree, former Mayor of Detroit and Governor of Michigan from 1897 until 1900. It had a basement, a first and second floor and an attic with one light bulb. Only occasionally did we venture into that spooky attic.

━

DAD WAS A grocer and owned and operated the third-largest grocery store in Pontiac. He built it himself, with help from his three brothers, in the depths of the Great Depression in the early '30's. Prior to that, aware that in business as in real estate, location-location-location was crucial to success, he operated an open air fruit and produce stand for a couple of years smack on the corner on the left side of the front of the house.

The City of Pontiac's Health department showed up one day and demanded he close down the operation. It seems there was no toilet facility or sink for workers to wash their hands. After Dad was ticketed, he appealed the Health Department's judgment to the Circuit Court. There he explained to the judge that employees (all of whom were relatives) went inside the house to use the facilities. Dad won the case and the ticket was dismissed.

But that was far from the end of the story—the City appealed the decision to the Appellate Court where the Circuit Court decision was overturned. As a result, Dad was forced to build a new store or be put out of business. It may be coincidental that this event coincided with Dad's joining the Democratic Party. He most likely realized he had to be "connected" with people who could help him in his efforts and business. Additionally, he must have felt the Democrats shared his values for helping people and being fair to everyone. I believe this was his first introduction into politics. From the artifacts that were passed down to me, it appears he became quite active. I have a letter from then-Governor G. Mennen Williams (in "Soapy's" trademark green ink of course) thanking Dad for providing "refreshments" at a fundraiser. There is a moral to this story: The City should never have screwed with K.J. Ritter!

While Dad was building businesses, as if Mother didn't have enough on her plate with a dozen kids, as a registered nurse she used her medical training to make sure we were all well fed and medically cared for. Mother ran our house "by the Book" yet somehow was funny and even sometimes delighted in original practical jokes. One April Fool's Day, she fixed biscuits for dinner. She put cotton balls in a few of them. I didn't get one, but it was hysterical when others bit into theirs. Of the dozen children, four of us were born in August, three early in the month, then a three-week drought. We noted that Dad liked to hunt and was often gone from time to time. In fact my younger brother Ed and I are the same age for three weeks. Moreover, the children born early in August had been conceived coinciding with his departure at the start of hunting season and those born later in the month matched up with his welcomed homecoming. My Mother and Dad—bless 'em—lived their commitment to faith and family, providing a Christian home and family structure for their children.

⌐

IN MANY WAYS, my young years were typical of other kids growing up in the '50s, but having eleven brothers and sisters certainly made for many memories. Once when my parents were away for a weekend, my oldest sister, Joan, was left in charge. That meant she was keeper of "the scandal sheet" taped to the icebox door. Every offense was written on the sheet for Dad's review. Lucky we had erasers. Still, one Saturday all of us kids were getting ready to go to a movie, and Joan told me I couldn't go, in punishment for some horrible offense or other. After yelling and crying, I finally came to my senses, snuck out of the house and had a great time at the movies watching the *Ten Commandments,* oblivious to the irony.

In the 1950s, Pontiac had great Memorial Day parades. Every kid in the neighborhood festooned the wheel spokes of their bike with red, white, and blue crepe paper. The best part was attaching a stiff piece of cardboard with a clothes pin to the back fender of the bike to make it click against the spokes and the faster the bike went the faster the clicks. We were so cool riding up and down Saginaw Street along the side of the parade just clicking away. If the cops noticed, they just looked the other way.

Of course with a clan as large as ours there were rules. At dinner, with everyone reaching for this and that on the table, a lot of glasses of milk were knocked over. Finally, Dad handed down the decree: "Milk will be served only after the meal is finished. All food has to make a full circuit about the table before anyone can begin to eat." Reasonable rules, but they could be bent if not broken with a little creativity. At the long-lasting holiday and special event meals, brother Tom would place a gallon of milk in the bathroom sink. Throughout the meal, the boldest kids would ask for permission to take a bathroom break. Problem solved... until someone tipped off Mother. For years I have had my suspicions who the mole was, but to this day she hasn't come forward.

Opening Christmas presents (or "Having the Tree" as we called it), was a wild and crazy time at our house. We had to wait until church and breakfast were over before the two sliding doors to the living room were pushed aside. It was an unbelievable sight: high piles of gifts sprawled across the room. Dad handed out presents one at a time, announcing which kid it was for. Only after all the gifts had been handed out could anyone open a gift. The wait was unbearable, until the moment the free for all began with wrapping paper flying everywhere, amid screams of excitement and delight.

Every Christmas proved again how amazing my Mother was. One summer I had asked her if I could have a Daisy Air Rifle for my birthday. She said she was sorry, but didn't think so. The following Christmas there, under the tree, was a Daisy Air Rifle for me. When I looked at her, she winked. I was totally amazed and excited. As I look back, she must of had kept a list throughout the year for each of the dozen kids.

⌐

DAD OWNED FOUR Ritter's Farm Markets. Four or five days a week, he drove to Detroit's Eastern Market to buy fresh vegetables and produce from local farmers. In those pre I-75 days, the only way to Detroit was down Woodward Avenue where Dad had the traffic lights timed and seldom caught a red light. I often went along with him to that terrific market, imagining all the way the taste when I would sink my teeth into the best hot dog in the world in a steamed bun topped with mustard and onions, followed by a gulp of chocolate milk. I also loved the horse-drawn fruit wagons that hoofed the streets of Detroit's residential areas house to house peddling produce. Their wagons had an A-frame down the middle so everything could be displayed on the two sides.

When we left the Market we would drive across town to the Detroit Union Produce Terminal on Fort Street. There, fruit and produce had been hauled in by refrigerated semi's or trains, mostly from California—oranges, peaches, sweet cherries, grapes, cantaloupes, tomatoes, etc. The Terminal was a very big time operation where all area supermarkets bought their fruit and produce, the only place where a retailer could have access to fresh fruit and produce.

Dad used to tell about an incident at the Terminal back in the early 1950s. All of the loaders and unloaders were Teamsters, as were most truck drivers. There was a huge push then by the Teamsters to sign up new members, including merchants. Dad stayed clear of these guys until one morning two large goons approached him and told him to show them his union card. He didn't have one. They gave him an application and watched while he filled it out on the spot and paid his dues. When he left the Terminal that morning he was a relieved, reluctant Teamster who still had his teeth.

All of us kids grew up working at the markets. In the summer of 1956, when I was eleven going on twelve years old, I started working at the Auburn Heights market on Auburn Road. I was paid one dollar a day, not bad for a kid—or so I thought. Each morning, Mother packed my lunch and I rode the Bee Line bus out to work, paying the fifteen cents fare each way. It finally dawned on me I was really making only seventy cents a day, so I asked Dad if he would pay my bus fare. He gently but clearly taught me that for the rest of my life there would be expenses like that I would have to bear. As if that helped.

~

WE ALL ATTENDED Catholic schools and in first grade I looked forward to the break after Christmas. But then my cousin Charlie Dean said something that ruined it for me. The way it happened, we were standing in line and Charlie whispered something to me. He said that the days off from school would be great and it was too bad we had to come back to school after Christmas vacation. Nobody told me that was the way it worked, that we had to come back and start school all over again after Christmas, devastating news to me.

Despite that setback, school was okay up through the fifth grade. That was when, in geography class, we learned that the largest lake in South America, located between Peru and Bolivia, was Lake Titicaca. I've always wondered how difficult it was for the nun to say that word. With our young bodies just awakening to life's cycle, we all wanted to go to Lake Titicaca. Oddly enough, we all received passing grades on that chapter's test.

In high school, class time became pure drudgery for me and it showed in my grades. Could I have been the only kid who never made the honor roll? I could have been inducted into the National Honor Society if they had let me double my GPA score. But in 1964, somehow, after my second year at summer school, I graduated.

I worked a couple of jobs up through the Spring of 1965 when I began working for Hartford's Roofing and Siding as a laborer. There was no roof-top delivery in those days. It was one eighty-pound package of shingles after another, balanced on your shoulder with one hand on the ladder rung, up, down, and up again. I also worked with the hot tar crew. The crew hauled a hot tar trailer to each site. The tar itself came in a round three-foot diameter roll which had to be chopped apart with an axe, thrown into the hopper using propane to melt the tar down. It was then pumped through pipes to the rooftop where it was poured into large buckets and dragged to the moppers who slopped it onto the roof itself.

Grueling and miserable as it was, it turned out to be the best job I could have had at the time because the hard labor beat me into the best physical shape of my life. Unbeknownst to me at the time, three weeks later, it would pay off in spades by making my Army Basic Training at Ft. Leonard Wood, Missouri, a little more bearable, although I admit that sets the bearability bar pretty low.

～

THE WAY IT happened, in August 1965, being the typical all-knowing nineteen-year-old smart ass, I decided to join the U.S. Army. I got the strange feeling that that news came much to my father's great relief.

I didn't own a car and so I asked my best friend, John Gibbons, for a ride to the recruiting office in Pontiac. I went into the recruiter's office while John stayed in the waiting area. I listened intently to the recruiter's very upbeat and exciting spiel of the good things that would come to me from joining the Unites States Army. He talked about a range of choices I could consider. Very quickly I found myself agreeing to a four-year enlistment to the United States Army Security Agency (USASA). But first, to be accepted for the ASA, I had a battery of tests to take. Not only that, I would also have to qualify for a Top Secret crypto clearance investigation conducted by the F.B.I.

That last condition drew me up short. All the sins, youthful indiscretions, and bad choices of my teen-age years (which were pretty tame, actually) flashed through my mind. How could I possibly pass an investigation by the F.B.I.? There goes my James Bond dream of only a few minutes earlier of becoming a top secret electronic spy, intercepting secret communications from countries around the world. But nonetheless I was hooked and excited.

Only after I signed the necessary papers did the recruiter ask me about my buddy John sitting just outside the door. Without missing a beat, he asked if I was aware of the Army's "buddy plan" whereby if two friends joined together they would be able to train together. Oh boy! I motioned to John to join us. I told him that I had just joined and with the recruiter's help gave a description of the ASA and its top-secret mission. I could tell John was very interested and when he learned about the buddy plan, he was hooked and signed up as well. (His mother never forgave me for taking advantage of John's spirit of adventure.) We were told to report to Fort Wayne in Detroit for our physicals and from there a train would take us to Fort Leonard Wood, Missouri for nine weeks of basic training.

My original goal was simple—to get out of boring Waterford. As for John, he was just giving a buddy a ride to downtown Pontiac. Next thing we knew, we're standing at a railroad siding in rural Missouri waiting for a bus to take us to Fort Lost-In-The-Woods. We were clueless about what lay ahead for us. Clueless. It was probably a good thing because had we known, maybe we would have made different decisions.

But we stayed the course and thus began *Den's Excellent Military Adventure.*

BASIC TRAINING BEGINS

The bus dropped about forty of us at the receiving station where an army sergeant was waiting. With a loud and hearty voice he introduced himself and ordered us into four lines. He paused and then said "I am your new mother. I'm not your fucking mommy—she's home doing the wash and fixing supper where she belongs. Understand?"

I didn't have to think long before replying, "Yes sir!"

Our new mother then told us that we were to march to an empty barracks to drop off our bags and relax before the G.I. Party was to begin. Everyone looked at each other and was excited—we're having a party. A Welcome-to- the-Army party. Was this gonna be a fun place or what!

Moments later the door burst open and in came several recruits with buckets, mops, soap and floor wax. Then a large pit bull started barking orders to start the party, ordering us what to do and how to do it. The pit bull said he would be back in one hour to inspect how the party was going. If the inspection failed we'd have to redo the entire party and that would mean we would most likely miss chow.

We did pass inspection and we did finally have chow.

The next morning we stopped by the barber for a haircut. Everyone entered the front door and exited out the back door. When John and I got into the shop and looked at the freshly shorn recruits, we knew what we were in for. We were not very happy about it. As I got in the chair I asked the barber to take just a little off the sides. No reply. In a couple of minutes it was over. As I rubbed my new slickly shaved bald head, the barber said, "Sorry, I misunderstood." I guess I shouldn't have also asked him if he was a licensed barber.

Every training day was just like the one before. Reveille at 5:00 a.m. The daily, two-mile morning run before breakfast. And off we went. But after about a quarter-mile at a gut-busting pace, men fell out and puked. And so it went, run, puke, run, puke, run and finally back to the barracks—except for the two dozen or so that didn't finish. And so it continued, as the fall-outs learned the art of the push-up.

The next run was to the chow line where skinny guys could have seconds and fat guys could not. The food was decent on a good day, but as for the bad days, let's not relive that all over again. Next, we lined up and ran to the athletic field for our daily phys ed.

Training was intensive. More like sadistic punishment. After a week of extreme physical abuse and incessant mental degradation, this nineteen-year-old know-it-all smart ass began to seriously question a decision made back in August. And what about my buddy John? How was he holding up? Oh, how I wished I had hitchhiked to Pontiac that fateful day and had not drawn him into this misery.

So it went, running everywhere. There was the three-mile out and three-mile back firing range and the grenade toss range. We did the belly crawl through mud flats under very low barbed wire with simulated mortar rounds exploding all around. There was the unexpected, as when a draftee shot himself in the calf with his M-14 rifle. The bullet traveled down through his leg and took off his heel. Some said it was an accident and some said it was all just to get out of the army. Only he knew for sure.

Finally, incredibly, Basic Training at last was over. We were given our leave orders, plane and bus tickets and pay. John and I ran (right up to the very end, we were still running) our asses off to the Post's bus station. There we caught the first bus to the St. Louis airport, overjoyed just knowing we'd never see Ft. Lost-in-the-Woods ever again. Homebound via Trans-World Airlines in time for Thanksgiving. How fitting.

FT. DEVENS

It was early December and after a glorious two-week leave home, I arrived at Ft. Devens, Massachusetts, northwest of Boston. I was here for advanced training in electronic surveillance techniques, various intercept methods and equipment, different types of code and four months of Russian language. What a change from Basic Training—no barking or screaming sergeants, no KP or fire watch and reasonably good food.

Training went well, although there was an awful lot to learn and retain. The difficulty I experienced most was an almost futile attempt trying to learn the Russian language written in the Cyrillic alphabet which had to be memorized. I had to be able to spell, pronounce/understand certain words whether in written or verbal form. I quickly discovered this was not "see Dick run after Jane." This was not conversational Russian. This was all military terminology, which made sense, because after all I was in the U.S. Army.

On Friday nights my friends and I would head out into the cold winter air and walk to the USO in downtown Ayer, a mile off Post. There was a nursing school not far from Ayer in the city of Lawrence. Most Friday nights you could expect a bus-load of student nurses to come down to the USO looking for soulmates. We soldiers, of course, were looking for something else. It was coke and cookies, but no alcohol allowed, and although that was strictly enforced, the occasional bottle of rum managed to make it in, wrapped in a jacket.

On one occasion we set such a bottle, covered with a jacket, on a bench that ran along an entire wall. But some-one moved the jacket to sit down and suddenly an unopened bottle of rum rolled off the bench onto the floor and broke. No one claimed the jacket and one by one we slowly got up and walked out, having just lost eleven dollars. It was winter and one of our group froze his ass going back to Post. I often wondered how long that jacket hung in the lost and found.

In early June 1966, school was over. I somehow managed to satisfy my Russian instructor and had passed my other tests. I anxiously awaited my orders to find out where I was being sent. Viet Nam had been on my mind for some time. My orders came through—I was assigned to the 4th USASA Field Station, better known as Kagnew Station at Asmara, Ethiopia. My orders required me to obtain a passport and to fly in civilian clothes when leaving Detroit for Ethiopia. I was going to the Horn of Africa.

I phoned home immediately and when I told mom the good news, I heard a huge sigh of relief. All of her prayers, novenas and rosaries had been answered. I went to get my passport and received it within ten minutes. I couldn't believe the Army's efficiency, a joy I was never to experience again. I jammed my duffel bag full and quickly went to HQ to pick up my travel allotment and plane tickets to Detroit and Ethiopia. Soon, I was on my way home and a two-week leave.

~

BACK IN WATERFORD, I slept in and ate lots of delicious home-cooked food. For more than a week I hung out with old friends, had a few beers together, and went water skiing several times. Three days before I was to leave for Africa, my younger brother Ed, who had been stationed in Germany with the Army, was discharged and came home. I hadn't seen him in three years. He was a pretty cocky kid and came home a mature cocky adult man. I had many questions for him about being in the service and he had some answers that proved to be prophetic.

Just before it came time to leave, I stopped over to see my shanty Irish Grandma Carry and other relatives. I looked in on my friends, at least those who were able to get out of the rack after the previous night's farewell mistake. I put on my civvies and mom and dad drove me to Metro Airport. Off I flew to Kennedy Airport, onto Rome and then to Athens, Greece, including an unforgettable fourteen-hour layover. Finally, late that night we left for my new home for the next eighteen months, Kagnew Station, Asmara, Ethiopia.

~

AS THE ETHIOPIAN Airlines Boeing 707 jet started its descent, I got my first glimpse of the dry and dusty countryside. As we taxied, to my right was a small terminal and I could see people, cars, trucks, a few horse drawn two-seat carts, and an Army bus. On the left side however, were a dozen or so wood and straw huts, most with wood stick fences, goats, a few cows, scantily clad men and women and lots of children wearing only cloth wrapped around their privates. That was cultural shock #1.

We got off the plane into very hot but dry temperature, unloaded our bags, went through customs, and were waved through. Our passports were stamped and the four of us boarded the bus for the twenty-minute ride to Kagnew Station. We drove through a part of Asmara proper, surprisingly very clean with wide boulevards, resembling a beautiful European city. I later learned that the city was designed, laid out, and built by the Italians when they colonized Ethiopia during the nineteen thirties and early forties before the British Army drove them out and Emperor Haile Selassie returned from exile to rule once again.

We were waved through at the main gate of the HQ complex. After reporting in, there were lots of papers to sign and then we were given our housing location. With an office clerk leading the way, we grabbed our gear and followed him to barracks "B".

All of the barracks were of WW II vintage. The clerk took us inside and showed each of us our bunks where we dropped our bags and then he gave us the fifty-cent tour of the station. It had a big mess hall, small PX, small hospital, and an Enlisted Men's club. Believe it or not, there was a movie theater and swimming pool. As we would soon see, there was even more.

On the morning of the third day we boarded a bus for the mile and one-half drive to Tract A, where the Operations Center building was located, a large single-story windowless brick building with what seemed to be a hundred antennas and two dishes surrounded by an eight-foot cyclone fence with three rows of barbed wire on top. Outside of the fence was a small café serving hamburgers, sodas, etc.

We went inside to the watch office to meet the Officer of the Day. He gave a full tour of the facility. There were several rooms we were not allowed into, too sensitive even with our top clearance because we didn't have a "need to know." Then we were turned over to a sergeant who gave us specific duties and schedules. There were three shifts—days, evenings and midnights—better known as "tricks". I started the next morning.

My first assignment involved collecting Egyptian diplomatic communications or "traffic" as it was called. Traffic was sent and received in five letter groups using encrypted teletype, encrypted phone, occasionally in "plain text" (verbal) and Facsimile. We searched the frequency spectrum twenty-four/seven using pre-determined grids seeking specific three-letter call signs. When a target call sign was discovered, the transmission method had to be identified and monitoring began with copying and recording of the frequency. The traffic was then delivered to the encryption room to unscramble and determine its value. Not everything was of consequence. By today's standards of heightened security concerns, this was low level intelligence gathering.

Within two months I was moved to the Russian desk. I began doing much the same as before, but this time I was monitoring and copying Russian military traffic. I now understood why the Russian language class was so important. At any given time we knew the location and/or movement of any military division. At first, this seemed interesting but before long it was actually very boring.

After another two months I was assigned to the Non-Morse Search and Development (NMSD) program. (The U.S. Military is big on initials.) At the time, Morse Code, both manual and electronic, was still widely used commercially and for low level military purposes, especially involving Third World countries. But that was changing. New electronic transmission techniques were beginning to appear within the frequency spectrum. Our job was to find new signals, ID them, and begin taping immediately. This was the meat of the NMSD mission. When a strange signal was discovered we immediately locked on and began taping the transmission while trying to identify it. Most times we were successful.

New technology was rapidly developing advanced signalization methods. On two occasions, despite our best efforts, we were unable to ID two new transmission signals. We were stumped. We requested NSA's help. Both times, NSA sent their techs over from Europe. We looked on with interest as they did their job. Impressive—they ID'd new encrypted equipment never used or heard before. It was both exciting and a big deal to have played a role in a breakthrough accomplishment like that.

Kagnew Station was located on a one-mile high plateau. Everything needed to run the station had to come by ship. All goods were trucked up the mountain over narrow roads from the Port of Massawa on the Red Sea. The Army also had a recreation facility there for R&R (Rest and Relaxation). My friend Duane and I decided to take a seven-day R&R to Massawa. I reserved a jeep, tent, sleeping bags, gas can, and other items and off we went.

It was a long hot drive down over a narrow dusty road full of switchbacks. It was a good idea to focus one's attention on staying well away from the edge.

We checked in at the R&R center and got directions to the North Beach area where we pitched the tent. It was a great location inasmuch as the average daily mean temperature was 125 degrees, but it cooled off considerably at night. We had a great time snorkeling, swimming, going to town and hanging out at the Rec Center. As we were skinny dipping our last night up to our calves, a group of strange fish began bumping our legs. Alarmed, we quickly reversed course. The next day we drove back up the mountain to a cooler Asmara. We turned in our gear, including the Jeep. The next day, our one week of freedom was already a distant memory and we were back to the grind.

Veteran's Day, November 11 of each year, is revered as a holy day of obligation with the military. It has always been celebrated by the military with great fanfare, but that year it was even more so for me, because the Emperor of Ethiopia, Haile Selassie I was coming to visit Kagnew Station. Even to the most jaded soldier, that was a huge honor and it was reflected in how the Post sparkled. Heck, even the rocks were freshly painted white (only a Vet can appreciate what that means).

The Emperor came in by chopper, landed on the parade field, and was escorted to Headquarters. Heavily armed U.S. and Ethiopian military assets were deployed both inside and outside the Post. American Embassy personnel had flown up from the capital, Addis Ababa. Everywhere you looked were VIPs, along with the Emperor's personal guard in full regalia. From my spot in the front of the crowd I was able to take unobstructed photos. When I first saw Emperor Selassie I was surprised—he was short, about five foot four inches. Even so, he was regal with his medals, honor awards, and his colorful sash. An exciting day for a kid from the sticks of Oakland County.

⌒

OFF DUTY WAS always great and spent mostly off Post, with lots of different things to see and do, but duty itself was becoming difficult to tolerate. With the arrival of the new Post Sergeant Major Shields, Army life at Kagnew Station began changing and not for the good. With his arrival, it became very strict, frustrating and irritating. Morale plummeted. The stateside spit-and-shine mentality had begun in earnest.

On one occasion I was in the otherwise empty mess hall

with two other guys getting a late breakfast. The door opened and in walked Sergeant Major Shields, short and stubby with a shaved head, and a cigar stub stuck in his mouth. He stood at the door, struck an authoritarian pose, hands on hips, and singled me out of the three of us from at least a hundred feet away. He bellowed, "Get a haircut." My reply, loud and clear, "Yes, Sergeant Major." He turned around and walked out the door as the three of us flipped him off. No matter how good his eyes might have been, he couldn't possibly have seen my haircut from one hundred feet. The personality of our base had changed totally almost overnight to one of typical Army harassment and I wasn't the only soldier who hated it.

All three tricks (work shifts) lived in the same barracks. Troops were coming and going while others were hanging out or sleeping. I was working trick two, the evening shift. Those working trick one had already left for work. The day sergeant came in to inspect each trick's area to make sure beds were made and all was neat and tidy. I was awake in bed but closed my eyes until he left. I then got up, dressed and went to the Enlisted Men's club to eat. That afternoon when I arrived at Track A, I walked past the posted "gig" list where all miscreants of the day and their dastardly deeds were listed. What? There was my name. My horrendous offense? Unmade bed. I stood there, guilty of an unmade bed?

I stomped into the watch office to explain to Sgt. Lucky that the gig was a mistake. I told him I was asleep in bed when the inspection occurred. The good Sgt. Lucky looked at me, dead serious, with his bloodshot eyes and said "Ritter, all I can tell you is next time sleep neat." I repeated to myself "sleep neat"?

The next morning I got up early, dressed, shaved and, of course, made my bed. I was a man on a mission as I walked over to the personnel office. I asked the clerk for Form 1049. I filled it out, checked it and handed it to the clerk who read it and looked at me puzzled, as if to say, "Are you sure?" What he probably meant was, "Are you nuts?"

I had just filled out a request to be transferred to Vietnam.

Everyone told me I was either crazy or stupid or both. They went on to say that I'd be denied anyway because no one with my MOS (military occupational specialty) had ever had a transfer request granted. Maybe so, but my request was approved and I had my orders within a week. When word got around, a stampede descended upon the personnel office to fill out Form 1049. It was hilarious; Sergeant Major Shields had started the world's second exodus. As for me, I was gone within two weeks.

I wrote my brother Tom and gave him the news. I asked him not to tell anyone and I'd call him when I got to New York. I flew out of Asmara in my civvies, passport in hand. We landed in Beirut, Lebanon and stayed overnight. The next morning we stopped in Ankara, Turkey to refuel and then flew straight to London. There I changed planes and headed to Kennedy. As it turned out, our plane was one of the first allowed to land because of a huge snow storm. It was late and nothing was flying out, so I slept on a row of chairs.

The next morning, I talked to Tom and a few hours later he picked me up at Detroit Metro Airport. When I walked into the house everyone was surprised and asked why I was home. At dinner, with everyone gathered around, I told them I was going to Vietnam, triggering the obvious questions— why, where, when, what for and how long. Then I dropped the bomb and said I had volunteered because it was what I wanted to do. Simply, I wanted to do my share for our country. "Jesus, Mary and Joseph," my Mother murmured. I knew right then she had already begun her regimen of prayers, rosaries, and novenas.

My leave ended on Sunday and that night my parents

drove me to the airport for a sad and uneasy goodbye. Mother was holding back tears and Dad's eyes were a little moist, as were mine.

Flying through the night I began feeling guilty for what I was putting the family through. Was I being selfish satisfying my quest at the expense of others? And then I started thinking about Vietnam and the nerves set in.

I landed at San Francisco airport where I took a cab to the huge Oakland Army Terminal. After I reported in, I was sent to pick up an issue of jungle fatigues, boots, etc. On the third day we were bused to Travis Air Force base, boarded a plane, and were off to Vietnam. We refueled in Guam and then landed at Subic Bay Naval Base in the Philippines and spent four days waiting for a flight out.

VIETNAM

We flew into Pleiku, in the central highlands of the Republic of South Vietnam.

The pilot cautioned it would be a high and quick descent to minimize the chance of being hit by enemy fire. We didn't know he was having fun with the new guys. Stepping off the plane, I was immediately overwhelmed by the oppressive heat and humidity and the most God-awful stench. Red dust everywhere cast a red shadow over everything. Walking down the stairs I saw several trucks carrying men wearing full fighting gear, rifles, grenades, rocket launchers, flak jackets, and ammunition. They looked rough; they had just come in from the field.

I stood at the bottom of the stairs, stunned, thinking, "Ritter, you dumb son-of-a-bitch, what have you done?"

I checked in at the flight desk, presented my orders, and asked where I could catch a flight to Phu Bai and the 8th Radio Research Field Station, I was told to report back in the morning but for now to go to the transit barracks for sheets and a pillow.

After I settled in, I went to the mess hall where I saw a sea of new dark green fatigues, men who had just arrived and were having their first meal. New arrivals were called "nubies." Seasoned soldiers liked to say, "These nubies were so new that they were still pissing stateside water." Then it occurred to me: so was I.

After I ate and returned to the barracks, I sat outside on a sandbag wall looking up at the stars, watching the constant night flares around the perimeter of the base, and the frequent muzzle flashes past the far end of the runway. Throughout the night the 106mm howitzers fired H&I (harassment and interdiction) shells into predetermined grids to harass "Charlie" to let them know of our vigilance. I did not sleep much that night. I tossed in my bunk, wired tight, nervous, over-tired, yet excited and praying for daylight.

Early the next morning I caught a C-130 and flew to Phu Bai, south of Hue, close to the South China Sea and below the DMZ (Demilitarized Zone).

⌒

WHEN I LANDED at Phu Bai, I walked over to the only building, a three-sided metal hangar, the open side facing the runway. Two grungy Marines with their gear lay there on a pile of flattened cardboard. For an instant I thought they were dead, and was relieved to see they were only napping. I found the sergeant in charge and asked where I should go. He glanced at my pristine green jungle fatigues, baseball cap, and shiny new jungle boots and, as he pointed the way, he chuckled and muttered, "new in Country."

I walked to the front gate which had a ten-foot high sandbagged tower. The entry was only one vehicle wide with thick sandbag walls on both sides and further secured with rolls of barbed wire. It was heavily guarded and if that wasn't enough, there were two eight-foot fences that surrounded the entire base, about twenty feet between them. The land in between was laced with mines. After the MPs told me where Headquarters was located, I picked up my life's possessions and headed there.

I handed my orders to the Company Clerk and the hour-long processing began with many forms to fill out. I was assigned quarters, issued an M-14 rifle, and was taken to my quarters in one of seven rows of wide, one hundred and fifty-foot long trailers attached end to end. Each row had a center aisle with rooms on both sides, each with two bunk beds and four lockers. The bunks were extra wide with thick mattresses, and best of all, the rooms were air conditioned. Did I hit the jackpot or what?

It was getting late when I met my roommates. One of them, Jim Fear, (an apropos name, being in a war zone) took me over to the mess hall to eat. I sat down with a loaded tray and noticed there were dead bugs in the bread. Before I could say anything, Jim laughed and explained that when the dough was being kneaded, bugs would fall from the lights above, so they were just mixed in, baked, and put through the slicing machine. He said don't worry they're dead, just pick em' out.

At orientation the next morning I was told I'd be going with two other men to Hill 180 as an intercept operator. At any given time three and sometimes four men would on be on the Hill. It was a 24/7 operation. I would be on the Hill three to four days at a time depending on activity and then we would return to the base camp for two days off.

Our mission was to continually search known frequencies used by the VC (Viet Cong) and NVA (The People's Army of North Vietnam) while at the same time searching the spectrum looking for NVA traffic. When found, we taped and tried to determine the method of transmission. The type of equipment used helped us determine a unit's size, from a squad up to a division level. I was told to expect lots of Morse Code traffic used by small VC and NVA units, but be vigilant for any UHF signals used at division level and record everything. I was also told that on the top of each shelf of our vital electronic equipment I would find thermite grenades. When activated, a thermite grenade would burn down through metal and destroy everything. I was to use these if the Hill came under attack and was in jeopardy of being overrun. Overrun. My butt tightened.

The next morning we were dropped on top of the hill and I started my first shift.

The operation area was small—one green metal Conex box structure ten feet by eight feet, seven foot high and full of equipment, some of which I'd used before. There, on top of the shelves were the thermite grenades. There was a small tent with five open sides, sandbagged walls waist high and four cots. A generator provided power. For our nature calls there was a "piss" tube fashioned out of two hand-held rocket canisters, but most impressive was our restroom affording a scenic view overlooking the South China Sea. It featured a plywood box with two stolen toilet seats, minus covers, nailed down. Before I left the Hill I fashioned an ingenious shower out of a fifty-five gallon drum and piping I "requisitioned" from the motor pool back at the base camp. The Marines were ecstatic.

⚊

I SPENT THE first day acclimating myself to the Hill, checking out equipment I wasn't familiar with and working side by side with the operator. I asked about food and was told the C-Rations were in the tent and to help myself. I opened a one-man meal box which had a can of peaches, a can of beans and franks, a four pack of cigarettes, pound bread the size of a tuna fish can, condiments and utensils. I asked John Hoyt where to heat the main dish. He laughed and reminded me this was a war zone and one has to be able to improvise so put it in the sun, so I did. My first C-Ration meal wasn't too bad. The liquid was water, but John told me a couple cases of soda and beer occasionally found their way up the Hill.

For some time, the nights were the worst for me. Being so high up, I could nearly see three hundred sixty degrees around me. Every night there were lots of flares and on occasion a fire fight off in the far distance. Bright green or white tracer bullets meant it was NVA using munitions provided by the Chinese. During the first night I heard 175mm howitzer shells whistle northbound overhead. That howitzer had an astounding range—up to twenty-five miles—and was fired from the 3rd Marine Division's Headquarters (3rd MAR DIV) basecamp next door to my base camp. It happened night and day, probably as fire support during an operation.

During my stint on the Hill, we were mortared once. No one was hit, but there was some damage. While down in the basecamp, we went on alert many nights, always around 2:00 a.m. to interrupt our sleep, forcing us to run for the trenches with our gear.

My time spent on Hill 180 was exciting but not as brutal as that endured by the battle-hardened Marines who had just been rotated back from the fighting near the DMZ, the Au Shau Valley to our west toward Laos, the many Ho Chi Minh trails, and the Marine base at Khe San. I was twenty-two at the time; these "kids" were eighteen or nineteen years old and they all had the thousand-mile stare.

On Christmas Day, 1967, I was transferred to the 175th Radio Relay Station at Bien Hoa Army base, thirty-five miles northwest of Saigon. There, the mission was much the same and I met up with a few friends from Ft. Devens.

On the night of January 31, 1968, I was assigned Sergeant of the Guard. I had just finished checking all guard posts making sure all were awake. About 2:00 a.m, all hell broke loose. B-40 Rockets, 122mm rockets and 60mm and 120mm mortars started hitting the Base, exploding in brilliant blasts. The Tet Offensive had begun.

Our choppers that weren't hit immediately lifted off and began their work. There was already heavy fighting at the front gate, nearly breaching it before the 101st Airborne repulsed the attack. Somehow, despite the danger, in a strange way it was like a Fourth of July fireworks display. Rockets rained from the Hueys, ricocheting back up. Cobras strafed the enemy and took heavy incoming fire. From the south side of the base, five hundred yards away, I could hear heavy machine gun and small arms fire where the 11th Armored Cav Division, better known as Black Horse, was located. Everywhere, the crack of AK-47 fire.

It went on for hours. Finally, after 10:00 a.m., the fighting halted. The mission of the Viet Cong and NVA had been to attack the Bien Hoa Air Base and blow up the fighter jets. But they made a tactical error—they had tried to go through the Army Base to get there and now at least two hundred thirty-six enemy lay dead outside the wire.

The next morning, two bulldozers scooped out a long, deep trench. After a search for weapons and intel, they pushed in the already bloating bodies and covered them up.

⌐

As my first tour of duty was ending, I signed for a second tour. After that six-month tour, I signed up for my third tour.

Two weeks before I was to leave, the Company was called

out for formation. The forty of us fell in and were called to attention. The Company Commander proceeded to introduce the new Command Sergeant Major. Unbelievably, it was the ghost of Kagnew Station, Command Sergeant Major Shields. From within the formation, the muffled sound of groans, including mine. It was obvious that others were familiar with him too. I couldn't have been more thrilled, knowing that in fourteen days I was leaving the military and all the Shields within it.

That was enough Vietnam for me. I was looking forward to getting on the Freedom Bird and going home.

⁓

WHEN I LANDED at Detroit Metro, I was surprised and happy to see a huge throng of family and friends to welcome me home. Mom was at the front of the crowd and gave me a big hug while I shook my smiling Dad's hand. It was such a huge relief to be home, but it took several weeks before it truly sunk in.

After bumming rides for a few weeks, I needed a car. My mother's cleaning lady, who reminded me of the "Little Old Lady From Pasadena," had her 1966 GTO for sale. I bought it for $1300, my first car and it was a screamer. When I started school in the Fall, I sold the GTO for $1400 and bought a VW for reasons that escape me.

I worked at the Huron Street Market for several weeks before I took a dive. I broke down and told my dad in the back room that I couldn't handle it anymore. I was weeping, but tried to hold back. I was a mess. I said the market was not organized; things were not tidy, neat or orderly. There were too many things coming at me, too much to handle. I had been in the Army too long and in Vietnam too long. The Army's structured environment clashed with my new-found freedom of mind. This was uncharted waters for Dad, and me, for that matter. He didn't know what to say or do for me but did suggest maybe I should see Dr. Pridmore, his primary. I did and we had a very long and helpful talk. Soon after, thanks to my cousin Bob Carry, I found a new summer job with the City of Pontiac in the Department of Public Works. As summer arrived, things slowly calmed down.

I felt that I needed my own place. Two friends who worked at GM had a line on a house and needed a thousand dollars share from me to seal the deal. My dad said instead I should buy the house have my friends pay rent enough to pay the mortgage. He loaned me the money and I became a landlord.

I knew I had to go to school, but with my high school grades, no way would I be able to get into the University of Michigan. Someone suggested Oakland Community College to improve my GPA so I enrolled and started classes the day after Labor Day. That holiday weekend, the girlfriend of John Kretsch, one of my renters, talked me into a blind date with her friend, Sandy Sinischo, a teacher living in Southwest Detroit. So I called, we talked and we doubled dated with my other renter/friend Ed Sommer and his girlfriend.

Sandy was beautiful, in every way. One thing about having been in the Army, especially a war zone, the real important things in life rapidly surface and become crystal clear. After our second date I knew immediately I was going to marry this woman.

I had known Sandy for seven weeks when I asked her to marry me. She said yes and we set the date for February 7, 1970 (exactly five months to the day we first met). The first semester at OCC I made the Dean's list and away I went for the next two years, earning the sixty hours needed to transfer to U-M. I was accepted and officially became a Wolverine.

In spring of 1973 I graduated from U-M with a degree in economics. At the same time, Sandy graduated from U-D with her masters. We bought a Volkswagen convertible here, arranging to pick it up in Brussels, and spent the summer traveling around Europe. We planned to stay in pensiones, but those boarding house arrangements didn't work out well. So, when we got to Zurich, Switzerland, we bought sleeping bags, a tent, cooking utensils, and other camping gear, including two air mattresses (in the Army we called them rubber ladies) and a camping guide to Europe and off we went. We put five thousand miles on the VW, driving from Belgium to Athens and back along a different route to Brussels. It was an incredible, unbelievable and romantic time for us.

Sandy had to be back by the end of August to teach. When we returned, the Detroit teachers went out on strike. Nine months later our daughter Sarah was born. A strike baby! When we returned I started working at the National Bank of Detroit.

In September 1975 my Dad died suddenly. At the funeral I met Jim Seeterlin, Supervisor of Waterford Township and a good friend of Dad's. I happened to ask him how the politics in Waterford were and told him I've always had an interest in government. That November, shortly after a Township Trustee on the Board died, Jim asked if I would be interested in being appointed to fill out the balance of that term. After conferring with Sandy, I told him yes. Being sworn in January of 1976 was my introduction to the world of politics.

In March 1976, I left the bank and went to work for Congressman Jim O'Hara of the 12th District (Mt. Clemens area) to be the Finance Director of his campaign for the U.S. Senate seat vacated by the legendary Phil Hart. Also running in that Democratic primary were Secretary of State Dick Austin, Congressman Don Riegle and James Elsman, a Troy attorney and political gadfly. Riegle decisively won the primary and went on to win the general election. As for me, I was out of a job.

I ran for Waterford Township Trustee in 1976 for a full

four-year term, won easily, and the Board remained Democratic.

In 1977, I opened a Ritter's Farm Market in White Lake Township. In March of 1978, I was asked to lunch by Jim Seeterlin and Jim Schell, the retiring Democratic Treasurer. They asked me to run for Township Treasurer, replacing Jim. The $24,500 salary with benefits was enticing and after talking with Sandy, who was very supportive, I agreed to run and the following August I sold my store.

A month earlier, on February 4, 1978 Sandy had given birth to our son Dennis M. Ritter II and we then hit the campaign trail. I say "we" because Sandy ran for and won a seat on the Oakland Community College Board of Trustees. She went on to win election after election until she chose to retire from the Board in 2014, having served an incredible thirty-six years on the Board.

The Board was only one of Sandy's many community services. She was very active with the Michigan Community College Association and its national counterpart, the Association of Community College Trustees. She was chair of the national Legislative Affairs Committee and testified before Congress on behalf of Community Colleges. She wrote papers that appeared in the Higher Education periodical that circulated the entire higher education community, not just community colleges. Highly regarded and respected around the country, in 1989 Sandy was recognized with the prestigious M. Dale Ensign International Leadership Award for the Association of Community College Trusties of the United States and Canada.

In early 1982, as Chair of the Waterford Democratic Club, a fellow from Lansing by the name of Bob Carr came to visit me. He was running for the 9th Congressional District seat he had won in 1978 but lost two years later.

Bob won his election and retook his old seat. He asked me

to be his campaign treasurer which I agreed to do. I continued in that capacity up through his run against Spencer Abraham for the U.S. Senate seat. Bob also hired Sandy as his District manager and she went on to run the District several years. But the clouds were gathering. In 1984, I was a Gary Hart delegate to the Democratic National Convention in San Francisco. That was also the year of the great Reagan landslide. My brother Tom decided to run as a Republican for Congress against Bob. I never knew of his decision until I read it in *The Oakland Press*. Obviously it caused a serious rift within the Ritter family. My brother Fred was running for re-election as Treasurer in Independence Township and I had my race in Waterford while Sandy was still running the District for Carr. Fred lost his election to a wallpaper hanger/salesman. I was re-elected by six hundred and fifty votes, Bob Carr won by about six thousand votes and Sandy's job was saved.

Bob lost his election to the U.S. Senate and Michigan and the 9th Congressional District lost the Chairman of the sub-committee on transportation who had been a huge supporter for our area on roads, bridges and transportation.

The Treasurer's job was full time and we made the best of it. In 1988, I decided to run for supervisor against the incumbent Republican supervisor. In a hard-fought campaign, I won the seat by a very respectful margin. Only later did I learn that winning the election was the easy part.

That first term was very busy and I had the support of nearly all department heads. The township Board remained Democratic. We made great progress. But in 1996 I lost my bid for re-election by three hundred sixty votes out of twenty-five thousand cast, to a nemesis on the township board. But in the 2000 election it was payback time as I ran the campaign of retired Waterford police sergeant Carl Solden and we crushed that same opponent after her one term.

IT WAS TIME to plow new fields—literally. So, I took a job at Bordine's Nursery selling trees and shrubs. I became a Master Gardener and earned my Michigan Certified Nurseryman certification, all while attending OCC, taking several classes in horticulture. I left Bordine's and started my design and landscape business, specializing in projects for senior citizens, removing overgrown shrubs and bushes replacing them with new low-maintenance materials.

IN 2003, SANDY and I sold our home in Waterford. A year earlier we had bought a two-acre parcel in the Historic District of the Village of Clarkston, which had a small house on it. We had the house de-constructed by an organization similar to Habitat for Humanity. They removed everything from the rafters to the foundation. As an added bonus, I was able to deduct fifty percent of the home's value on my income tax. In April 2005, we started building our new home with me as general contractor, and moved in that December.

IN 2008, VILLAGE Manager Art Papas, after forty-six years of impeccable service, announced his retirement. The previous October, Art had me appointed to the Planning Commission. Meanwhile the search began for his replacement. I was asked by several friends, as well as Sandy, to apply. I was appointed by City Council and started June 1, 2008, before retiring in 2013 after five very tumultuous years of the Great Recession during which we managed to keep the books balanced.

There was a certain irony with Dad's death in 1975 and

yet another example of how a bad time in life somehow opens the door unpredictably to something positive. That chance encounter with Township Supervisor Jim Seeterlin, deflected my career path to the political arena. Dad's most precious legacy for me was his highly respected name and he would have been delighted how it all worked out for his son.

7

HAVING WHAT YOU SHARE, KEEPING WHAT YOU GIVE AWAY
by Bob McGowan

"I have a theory regarding angels that it pleases me to believe. It's that often, in our time of greatest need, someone unlikely and unexpected will be there to help us. This seems to happen most frequently when we are young, because that's when we typically most need to be rescued."

SOMETIME IN THE mid-1970s in a train car in Algeciras on my way to Sweden from Morocco, I was sitting opposite several Arab men. They looked to me to be day laborers, perhaps Algerians, dressed in thin polyester trousers and rumpled cotton, tunic-type shirts, on their way to employment in France. They were rail-thin, the four of them, and their eyes glinted as from cataracts.

I had managed to buy a couple of liters of water in the station, and proffered a bottle. They smiled, thanked me, asked a couple of polite questions in French—where I was from, where I was headed—then continued talking in Arabic among themselves. After a time, leaning against each other, they took a nap.

Reluctant to pay train station prices, I had purchased only a little food: a roll, a bit of cheese and a small sausage, and, since I was ravenous, surreptitiously downed my meager provisions, not feeling I had enough to share among four other people. A while later, my cabin mates awoke and took down hampers of food from the overhead bins—a veritable feast of freshly-baked flat bread, several kinds of cheese, olives, ratatouille, cured meat, dates, sweets—and offered me some of everything. I was humbled and profoundly moved. That moment I vowed always to share whatever food I had, and have tried to extend sharing to most everything I do or own.

Years ago I recounted this incident to my stepson who more recently told me that it was the most important thing I ever taught him. I have included it in a book I'm writing about sharing as a meditation. Its one-liner takeaway is: *You only truly have what you share, and you only keep what you give away.*

⌒

IN 1990 MY wife Barbara and I moved to our current home in Clarkston, Michigan, on the core property of an 1850's dairy farm, called, for as long as anyone can remember, Bittersweet Farm, with barn, stables and other outbuildings. Since form follows function, and not wishing to maintain the place purely for aesthetics, I wanted to put the farm to some agricultural use. So I proposed to a garden club that was just forming that we start a vegetable garden as a community service, and donate the produce. That we did. And although the original garden group disbanded from attrition, the project continued, using Master Gardener volunteers as labor, with distribution provided by Gleaners Community Food Bank of Southeastern Michigan. Year 2016 is Bittersweet Farm Plant-A-Row

Community Garden's twenty-fifth year of operation. I calculate that our deliveries of organically-grown vegetables to the food bank have averaged around two thousand pounds a season, with a high of over five thousand pounds. Simple math brings our grand total to fifty thousand pounds over the life of the garden.

I've talked about my train episode and the garden because I wanted to explain what has shaped me philosophically and, specifically, what has lead me along the path that includes meeting every Monday morning with ten simpatico retirees, all politically progressive—that is, people who believe that government should play a strong, positive role in the lives of its citizens.

(On the societal level, this means helping secure the maximum good for the citizenry as set forth in our Constitution, a British ideal dating to the Magna Carta. On the level of the individual, as a French, Rousseau-ian ideal, good springs from an individual's maximum freedom as guaranteed in our Bill of Rights. Our government combines and balances these two ideals. Recently, our state and national governments have tipped in favor of the rights of the individual at the expense of the commonwealth. That's why, for example, in some municipalities, people have the right to carry guns, even into taverns.)

But this sounds more focused than I feel in setting forth a mini-memoir. My wife Barbara (without whose partnership I have no idea if or how this story would have unfolded, on which I elaborate in the Acknowledgments section later in this book, along with thanks to others) tells me that, when she was a girl living in Toledo, Ohio, she would ride her bike in neighborhoods she had never visited, becoming intentionally lost, then enjoy finding her way back home. Writing this memoir seems like a similar adventure, getting lost in the story. Finding my way back to "Home" in this case would be my Monday morning coffee klatch where I would share this memoir.

"Share" is the operative word with my coffee folks, as everyone in the group tells his or her stories. Because all the members are good listeners, taking the floor is a pleasure. They all seem to know, as the Vietnamese Zen Buddhist monk Thich Nhat Hanh says, that, "The most precious gift we can offer anyone is our attention." We seem at this point to have thematically re-boarded that Spanish train, on the topic of giving and sharing. So I want to give the group—and posterity—a story or two here that I hadn't recounted. Often the stories I've lived, those that are most significant to me, are, at the same time, the most mystical or dreamlike. First, though, a prelude to those stories.

⁓

WHEN YOU GET to a certain age, you stop being surprised when you belatedly comprehend how much your life was changed by a totally unpredicted event that occurred years—if not decades—ago.

One such seismic shift came when I was a youngster in Rochester, Michigan, although I really didn't recognize the import until many years later. I lived in Rochester from the time I was in the fourth grade, my parents having moved there after my father finished his tour of duty in the Korean War. Rochester was, and is, nestled a valley between two hills, the larger one to the south. As a kid, I loved returning home in the back seat of our car and seeing the lights of the town down below.

The area was mixed agricultural and industrial, bordered on the south by Ferry-Morse Seed Farm; to the north by a factory, National Twist Drill; to the east by Van Hoosen Farm and Yates Cider Mill; and to the west by Great Oaks Stock farm and the Golden Guernsey Dairy. Only the cider mill is still operational.

Our house was on the north end of town on the second-to-last street. Walking from home, if I headed south down the alley, I'd be downtown with its three hardware stores and the D&C dime store with its wood floors—that was where they roasted Spanish peanuts I'd buy for fifteen cents a quarter pound, still hot from the roaster. If I headed north, I'd be in open fields within a block, where I'd hike, explore and build forts. It was a great place to grow up.

I had a buddy dog, Prince, owned by the neighbors catty-corner across the street. Prince was half collie and half German shepherd, with the best qualities of each. When I came out our front door, he'd stand up on his porch. We'd meet in the street, and if I went left to town he'd follow me half way down the alley and then go back home. If I turned right, he knew I was headed for the fields or down the railroad track, and was with me for the duration. And tough? I saw him defeat a full German shepherd. He was a good friend.

Life was good, maybe idyllic, until high-school, where conformity was the rule—if one didn't wear white socks one was sub-human. Something was wrong with this, but I didn't know what. I wanted to be popular, but I was awkwardly immature. And why shouldn't I be well-liked? My mother loved me unconditionally, didn't she?

That was when something unanticipated and miraculous happened. A college came to Rochester. That institution turned out to be Michigan State University–Oakland, short-handed to MSUO, now Oakland University. MSUO was the Honors college for Michigan State. I was seventeen years old my entire first semester, amidst students from all over the country and the world. Sock color was optional. I loved the place.

Around that time Rochester began to expand, and to increase its tax base. That came at a high cost, to me at least. Many of my favorite haunts were razed. The worst, and the last straw, was the old people's home downtown, a mansion on a wooded lot surrounded by a stone wall. To my eyes, it reflected Rochester's character and quality, and relieved its cheek-by-jowl commercialism. It was torn down. I was so devastated that I turned my back on Rochester, and until I began to write this reflection, wouldn't let myself dwell on it since then.

In 1963, when I was halfway through college, my courses had become meaningless to me, for whatever reason. What was I doing in "The history of English architecture, from 1550 to 1850"? On the other hand, I liked French and felt I needed a complete immersion experience. So I did what seemed the sensible thing to do—I dropped out.

But I had very little money, despite having worked all summer as a card-room manager at a country club and having unloaded produce trucks at the A&P food market. I'd be up at five a.m. to unload the truck until noon, then drive 45 minutes to the club where I'd work from one in the afternoon to sometimes one in the morning, then be back at the grocery store the next morning. One night, returning from the country club, I fell asleep at the wheel and took out the side of my beloved Austin-Healey Sprite, which now exists only as an image in the montage on the inside of the covers of this book.

With what little money I ended up with—not enough for a round-trip ticket and travel expenses—I used to get to New York City to look for a job on a steamship headed for Europe, thence to France. While staying with a buddy, I applied to steamship companies for work, only to be told I had to have seaman's papers. When I approached the union for seaman's papers, they said I first had to have a job on a ship. Years later,

I realized that I probably could have broken this nasty hiring circle by greasing a strategic palm. I had much to learn about the ways of the world.

New York City is an expensive place, and I was going through my funds at an alarming rate. It was out of the question to head to Europe on a one-way ticket and rely on my parents to foot the bill for my return. So I bought a train ticket to Quebec City. I had never been there, didn't know anyone, and had no idea what I'd do when I arrived. I only knew that French was the *lingua franca*.

The trip was remarkable, passing through Vermont and Maine with foliage in full, blazing, psychedelic color—it was, after all, the Sixties. I stared out the window in awe when the train stopped at the Canadian border and the immigration officials went from car to car checking identification. I felt well prepared, having a passport for my anticipated trip to France. I was asked the usual questions: Where was I going in Canada, what was the purpose of my visit, how long was I going to stay. My reply: I'm going to Quebec, don't know what I'll be doing, and not sure how long I'll be there.

The official's face hardened and he sat down beside me. He grilled me for a good twenty minutes. Before long, I realized I was in danger of being put off the train, so I did some fast talking. I explained how I was in the middle of my university education and needed some direct French language experience. No reaction from the stone-faced official. My next ploy was to mumble something about perhaps taking some courses. That elicited a good news/bad news reaction. The good news was that I would get two weeks grace to get enrolled as a student at Laval University. The bad news was, if I wasn't enrolled within those two weeks, I'd be deported.

The prospect of possible deportation tends to focus the mind sharply. At least it did mine.

I arrived at the Quebec train station, had the cab driver take me to a cheap room, and, the next day, enrolled in the *premaitrise* (pre-teaching) program at Laval University, signing up for six courses—about the last thing I wanted to do. However, one of my fellow students, a woman from Elyria, Ohio who became my girlfriend, told me about a new, small professional theatre, Le Theatre de l'Estoc, that was looking for a stagehand. I went to take a look.

It was a beautiful little place, sharing a wall with the iconic Chateau Frontenac, heavily funded by the government, and run by a few young, brilliant, recent fine arts conservatory graduates. I applied for and got the job, having learned just enough French in high-school and my then two years of college. My girlfriend was the only other English-speaking person in the theater.

Now happily immersed in French, I dropped out of my courses at Laval. Marc Dore (still a good friend and whose book on theater improvisation I'm translating into English), was a professional mime, classically trained in France. He was also an instructor of stage movement, and was based at the theater. He gave me free mime lessons when mime was still cool, back before street mimes ruined the art by annoying their audiences.

This is where the dream-like, surreal part begins.

One afternoon during mime practice, a call came in from the Capital Theater in downtown Quebec, the city's venue for major theatrical productions. They were looking for extras for a performance of *Le Mariage de Figaro*, not Mozart's opera but rather the play by Pierre Beaumarchais. Starring in the production would be the great French actor, Jean-Louis Barrault. Marc and I immediately accepted roles as extras.

At the theatre we were shown to the dressing room and given our costumes and wigs for supporting roles as judges, underlings of the chief judge with the speaking role. Our in-structions were brief and specific: each of us would walk be-side the main judge. That was it. Finally, on cue, we took the stage. Adding to the unreality was that I was extremely near-sighted, and wore Coke-bottle-bottom thick glasses that I had had to remove, so everything was a blur.

At this point in the story the reader might expect a dra-matic turn, some on-stage disaster, but no, the production came off flawlessly. That's the thespian promise to the audi-ence, that the cast and crew will remain in control of the dra-matic experience, that the audience can suspend disbelief and enjoy the world of the work.

After our curtain calls, I got to meet and shake hands with Jean-Louis Barrault, regarded as the Sir Laurence Olivier of French theater. I had seen Barralt's marvelous performance in the film masterpiece, *Les Enfants de Paradis* (*Children of Paradise*). Meeting the master was a heady experience for a 19-year-old aspiring actor. I know it all happened—I lived it—but it still seems to have been in a parallel universe.

During the seven months I worked at Le Theatre de l'Lestoc, disaster did strike during two performances of one play. The play, part of an evening of one-acts, was *Conversa-tion Symphonietta,* by an absurdist playwright, Jean Tardieu. The play consists of everyday, banal conversation scored like a choral piece, with sopranos, altos, tenors, and basses. It's all quite formal, the performers in tuxedos, playing it straight. The eight cast members walk in, sit in unison, and begin warming up—mi, mi, mi; fa, fa, fa; so, so, so. Then the conduc-tor (a real one) enters, also in a tux, and the warm-up ends. The conductor raises his baton and the piece begins: "Hello, sir, how are you today? I'm fine, madam, how are you?" And so forth. There are solos, duets, full conversational chorus-es, crescendos, diminuendos and the finale, all consisting of mundane speech. Very good fun, a real audience pleaser.

What no one in the company knew was that the conductor was epileptic. During a performance of the play, around the middle of its run, the conductor began to sag. He steadied himself at the podium, rubbed his forehead, and tried to carry on. Finally he collapsed into a full-blown seizure, convulsing and groaning. Down came the curtain. Fortunately, there was a doctor in the house, and the conductor was ultimately okay. But it was terrible witnessing a real-life crisis curtailing a performance in a small, intimate professional theater. But there were other one-act plays on the bill and, in the tradition of the theater, the show went on.

Sometimes a particular play is jinxed. Weeks or months into a long run, a cast may become bored or complacent, and bad things can happen. To spice things up a bit, the actors may play tricks on each other. For instance, just as an actor is walking onto the stage, another cast member may look aghast at his head, as though the first actor's wig is crooked. The intent is to make the actor lose focus, to drop out of character, a major no-no in the theater. But sometimes lapses are spontaneous. Late into the run of that same one-act play at l'Estoc, the one with the unfortunate conductor, something happened that struck the cast as funny, perhaps the mispronunciation of a word. At any rate, someone started to giggle. Then another member giggled. Try as hard as they could, they couldn't stop. It was infectious and it was a disaster, breaking a compact with the ticket-buying audience. To everyone in a theatre company, such a breakdown is horrible. Your hair stands on end and you feel ill in the pit of your stomach. (Someone defined *terror* as recognizing a great danger, such as an approaching ravenous beast—*horror* is when the beast grabs you.)

⌐

GOING EVEN FARTHER back in time, my 1961 Austin-Healy "bug-eye" Sprite could be a blog entry on how cars I've owned have let me down in direct proportion to how much I liked them. And I really loved my Sprite. It was black with rolled and pleated camel-colored upholstery. Its black color made it look less squat than others of its breed, and it handled like a dream, squeaky-tight steering and suspension. It could take a turn as though it were on rails.

I enrolled in Oakland University which had just opened its doors virtually next door, so I lived at home and commuted to school, thus requiring reliable transportation. I hadn't yet heard it said that an English sports car is for people with a surplus of time and/or money, that it's more of a hobby than a conveyance. I had asked the previous owner if it had been raced, to which he replied in the negative. It wasn't until a few weeks into my ownership that I noticed the outline of racing stripes under its black paint job. Mechanically, however, it seemed to run just fine. The problem was that its Lucas electrical system was notoriously failure-prone. With my Sprite, the issue was moisture. If it was raining, had rained, or was going to rain, or even particularly humid, it wouldn't start. I'd have to roll it down our driveway, put it in second, and pop the clutch. If that didn't work, I'd head it down the hill in front of the house, and jump in. No luck, and I'd push it back up the hill and do it again.

This went on until I went to New York and, eventually, to Quebec City. I left the car and payments in the hands of my father. Some months later, around Thanksgiving, I think, I hitch-hiked back to my parents' home in Rochester and drove the Sprite the 750 miles back to Quebec.

My girlfriend's girlfriend's boyfriend, Hugues Roy, had

the room next door to mine two flights above the Restaurant Buade, across from the cathedral in the historic district. Because my check from the professional theatre where I worked was ten dollars (!) a week, exactly the same as my weekly room rent, there wasn't much left for food. I had sent for and sold much of my stamp collection which yielded a little cash, but I barely had enough money for bread and peanut butter. I remember early in my stay, before moving to my room over the restaurant, going three days without food. So Hugues, a student at Laval University in English and himself living on a shoestring, often shared his meager meal with me. This was typically head cheese and blue cheese on a baguette. Hugues loved cars and it was for him that I had brought the Sprite to Quebec, as a bit of a payback. I turned over the keys and didn't see him again for a week.

In French, Hugues's name is pronounced, approximately, "ewg rwah." In English, it's a much more pleasant "hew roy"— very Scottish-sounding. (I wonder if that's why he became an English major.) His home, a large, white clapboard house where he lived with his mother and four sisters, was in Vemi Ridge, a tiny town whose major industry was asbestos mining. Their home also housed the town post office run by the family. His father, who had worked in the mine, saved enough money to purchase a fleet of trucks, then sold the trucks to buy a grocery store, his life's ambition. When a strike hit the mine, he refused no one credit, went deep into debt, and lost the store. So he went back to work in the mine and, to repay his creditors, he augmented his income by fabricating large, canvas air filter bags. He died of asbestosis at a young age long before I met Hugues, and yet he remains one of my heroes.

By the time I had been in eight stage events at the university and several more in community theater, I was considering going into acting professionally. My most significant role was that of Tom, the son, in Tennessee William's *The Glass Me-nagerie*, a juicy part indeed. By all accounts I did all right. Still, I didn't pursue an acting career in large part because people's praise was too important to me. I feared that working for audience adulation would be highly retrograde to my ego.

So I put the theater aside and finished my B.A. in English and French, and went on to do a Master's Degree in English, since literature and writing were among my great loves. I taught for nine years, then broke into advertising, a plausible way of making a living as a writer in the Motor City. (There were teaching adventures aplenty, but for another time, another place.) As for the advertising business, there's plenty of ego involved, but, because there's a defined product or service for a client, it's at one remove from the fame game. I remained in advertising for some thirty years until my retirement. Along the way I was a creative director, and, for about a nanosecond, had my name on the door as a partner until we merged with another larger, more established agency, and assumed their brand while ditching my name.

⌇

MY INTEREST IN languages has, on occasion, taken a serious—that is to say, academic—turn. I developed a proficiency in generative philology, that is, the extrapolation of macro-linguistic patterns and principles from small strings of language. A mouthful, yes, but it has its analog in science, where it is shown that a thorough understanding of a single organism can presuppose and illuminate a wide range of species—also a mouthful. Like so many scientific breakthroughs, my philological theory has its roots in field studies.

For example, in several grocery stores, I noticed displays of patio furniture. There would be a round table with an umbrella surrounded by several chairs. I would see customers sit in the chairs as a respite from shopping. It seemed that always, nearby, there would be at least one shopping cart with a sign prominently displayed, "No nios en la canasta."

Interesting. So, I would do some quick analysis and would conclude that nios, obviously, is the Latinate form of the number "nine," while canasta, from the game, must be a portmanteau term signifying all card playing. Hence the sign just had to mean: "No nine-person card games." If my translation was correct, why then, in a single phrase, the store was able to forestall crowding around the table, while at the same time keeping customers from taking advantage of the patio furniture display.

That should be sufficient proof that my approach to linguistic analysis at least clearly demonstrates that I have virtually no working knowledge of Spanish.

~

AN INCIDENT TEN years ago, before I retired, reflects the daily-ness of my life back then, the dominant activities being gardening and commuting to the advertising agency. Some functions you perform so many times you could do them blindfolded, if it weren't for the driving. And the forgetting.

I was half way down the gravel road that leads from the farm before I remembered the groundhog I'd trapped in the garden the night before. Most people shoot the beasts, and I rather wish I had, although I'd vowed that no animal on the farm would die by my hand. So I turned around, drove back to the corn crib and picked up the live trap with the live animal in it. I also grabbed a broom and then headed back out.

The stench of the animal and the trap filled the car, like the worst cage in a bad zoo. Five minutes southeast of Sashabaw Road along a wood-lined stretch of I-75, I pulled over, opened the back of the Jeep, picked up the broom, and took out the trap. I set it in some low weeds just off the paved shoulder. I opened the cage door and propped it with the broom and moved behind the trap, knowing from experience that groundhogs always sit on the release pan until they see the trap is open. It is then that they realize that I'm not between them and their freedom.

The liberated critter shot out and disappeared, leaving behind only a wake of waving weeds and the distinctive odor. I put the stinking cage back in the Jeep, opened wide all four windows, and continued on to a Starbuck's, then Bally's Fitness for exercise, and finally on to the agency.

The next day the car still reeked and no amount of simple ventilating the Jeep could kill the odor. Yet another good deed punished.

Notwithstanding the never-ending bouts with groundhogs, living in the country and raising nutritious vegetables for our own consumption and for people I'll never meet has rewards beyond measure. I recall one night I went out in the fading twilight to harvest tomatoes, zucchini, and yellow squash that the Master Gardeners hadn't picked. Wearing my Indonesian batik robe and drenched in sweat, I worked the rows until I had filled six banana boxes full of produce the Gleaners would collect at 6:00 A.M.

For some reason, the words of mobster Hyman Roth, in one of the *Godfather* films, came to mind. Roth has just learned that his man Mo Green has been whacked, and his stoic comment is, "This is the life we have chosen." Here I was, fresh off releasing yet another groundhog and stumbling around in a dark garden over zucchini lying in wait like so many alligators. I thought, Isn't fifteen years of this enough? That was ten years ago. Yes, I know that if you're not doing something joyfully, why do you keep doing it? Because this is the life I have chosen.

⌒

MY CONCERN WITH ego, beginning with myself relative to the universe and especially as I relate to other people, dates from the time I was fifteen years old; it includes dropping out of the Episcopal Church where I had been a choir member and acolyte. I couldn't reconcile Jesus' teaching—that we should love our neighbor as ourself—with church doctrine that seemed contradictory. Jesus the teacher (rabbi) said, according to the synoptic scriptures, that we should feed the poor and heal the sick. Then, especially in the Gospel according to John, we're told that all we need to get to heaven is to believe in Christ as God. (I examine this contradiction in a book I'm writing.)

Also, beginning many years ago, I developed a long, continuing interest in Buddhism that stresses the importance of breaking down the separation of self from others. (*Have you heard about the Buddhist who asked a hot-dog vendor to make him one with everything?*) This, too, is a major topic in my forthcoming book. Of course, Jesus' teaching that one should love one's neighbor as oneself, and eliminating the difference between the self and others, are effectively the same thing. It just happens that both are ultimately unachievable. However, it's the trying, I believe, that holds salvation, and I realize what a long, long way I have to go. I should by now have at least become philosophically centered.

These are the costs one bears from viewing life as a path, a process of becoming, instead of maintaining faith in a doctrine. Now, nearer every day to the end, I grow tired, and I also grow in understanding the appeal of salvation through death-bed conversion, something I had always scorned.

Fact is, I realize I'm becoming more codger-like every day. I find myself turning indignant over issues I thought I had come to terms with decades ago. For instance, I'm increasingly intolerant of fundamentalists' literal interpretation of the Bible. I think about the story of Noah's good friend God becoming angry with mankind and killing them (us), off, except for Noah, his family and some animals. How do you explain that to your kids? How about: The Bible tells us God is loving, but maybe he had a few too many drinks, got angry, and destroyed most of humanity. God may have been great, but good? To compound matters, they make coloring books of the Noah story for children.

I do have a theory regarding angels that it pleases me to believe. It's that often, in our time of greatest need, someone unlikely and unexpected will be there to help us. This seems to happen most frequently when we are young, because that's when we typically most need to be rescued. As we mature, our ability and opportunities increase for us to perform as angels to others. I see that as an obligation. In the following escapades, though, I was on the receiving end of an angelic act by someone else.

Angel One. In 1968 when I was twenty-four, on the first of six trips to Europe, I did a lot of hitch-hiking. Hitching in France from Carcassonne to Marseille, I caught a ride from a Fix beverage truck driver who was taking a load of empty soda and beer bottles back to the warehouse in Marseille. At Marseille, he would get a room near the warehouse, then leave the next morning after his truck was loaded.

A few minutes after climbing into his truck, I asked him how far he was going. That depends, he said, on how good a talker you are. Seems he had been on the road for thirty-six hours, and was worried about falling asleep at the wheel. If he couldn't make it, he'd get a room before he got to Marseille. This was all in French, of course, and I proceeded to tell the story of my life, any jokes I knew and could translate into French, and asked him perhaps a hundred questions. I sang

French songs, and he joined in.

We stopped at a truck stop for a simple dinner, then got back on the road. Somewhere outside Marseille, I reached for a cigarette in my sport jacket pocket, and, to my horror, no sport jacket. I had left it back at the truck stop along with my passport, wallet, and all my money. The driver pulled into the warehouse and bribed the dispatcher with a few packs of cigarettes to immediately unload the cases of empties and reload the truck with full bottles while he and I had coffee at a nearby caf. Then we walked back to the warehouse, got into the truck, and he drove and drove, me still talking all the way. After several hours we reached the truck stop. There, to my great relief, my jacket, passport and wallet had been kept safe.

We then continued on the road toward Carcassonne where I had already been, so he dropped me off near Avignon, which I had wanted to visit anyway. That driver must have been up at least fifty hours—amazing even for an angel. All I could do was thank him.

Angel Two. While staying at a youth hostel in Amsterdam I got a case of crab lice from the bedding, no carnal intermingling involved. Because the lice's provenance was boring, I have never written about it until now. But there I was, still itching and miserable after I arrived in Landskrona, Sweden, where I would work at my Swedish buddy Sven's greenhouse. There I met his cousin, a tall blonde woman, at a Swedish funeral, in a scene right out of a Bergman film. She worked for KLM and I had a date with her the next evening across the straits in Copenhagen. While staying at Sven's, I had tried ridding myself of the parasites by bathing, and surreptitiously applying alcohol, vinegar, anything I could think of, all to no avail.

Needless to say, my condition, in all good conscience, would have limited the cousin's and my range of activities. Back at the youth hostel the day before my date, while chatting with a simpatico fellow traveler as we sat on the hostel's front steps, I confided in him my predicament. He loaned me his tube of Kwel cream with the assurance that it would take care of my problem. One application and, like magic, I was vermin-free. Just to be clear, the angel here was the guy who just happened to be there and gave me the Kwel, not the young woman. Although she was lovely.

Angel Three. Back in the 1970s I wanted to show Quebec City to my then-fiancé Ingrid and introduce her to my friends there. We only had three days, but we set out in my VW beetle on that monster of a road, Highway 401. Somewhere south of Montreal in the middle of nowhere the VW slowed until finally we limped off the freeway at about five miles-per-hour and somehow crept to a gas station.

It was a late Saturday afternoon. None of the gas stations could look at the car, and the VW dealership was closing and wouldn't be open until Monday. We'd have to find a room and stay over until the dealership opened, and that would foreclose on our short vacation. Finally, someone I talked with mentioned a Mr. Innis, a semi-retired VW mechanic who lived nearby and worked out of his garage.

We found his place and rang his doorbell. He emerged from his house and we explained our predicament. A large German man with hands the size of hams, he listened to the engine and pronounced it in need of a valve job. Pushing the car into his garage filled with boxes of greasy used parts, he began work immediately. Inside of half an hour he had pulled the engine. Soon he had removed the head from the block and extracted the valves, one of which had a hole in it half the size of a dime. It was late and, saying he'd finish up the next day, drove us to a nearby cheap motel, and told us he'd pick us up tomorrow. The next morning he drove us back to his place where he had already found a used valve and had ground it to seat perfectly. Then he reassembled and installed the engine. I believe he charged us twenty-five dollars. I think Mr. Innis was an archangel.

~

THERE ARE, HOWEVER, areas where angels aren't of much help— aging is one of them. I might do a blog called, "I'm Not Aging Well." A sort of life-progress-report-cum-confessional, the blog would consist of musings on personal age-related top- ics, a springboard for some of my own personal and humor- ous foibles and failings. I would be taking on faith, or on gut, as we old ad men used to say, that men in my demographic group might relate to a few things I've been dealing with. Like where I've fallen short of standards I had set for myself. Much material to be mined, here.

One blog entry might be my somewhat mystical belief that whatever negative feeling or opinion I have about someone will instead be visited upon me. For instance, in California around 1979-80 when I was running seven miles a day, a cli- ent and frequent running buddy would refer to an overweight woman runner as "thunder thighs." It does me no credit to confess I thought at the time that his ridiculing her was hu- morous. It isn't such a big laugh now that I have gained a hundred pounds and can't run ten paces. Also, I blush when I recall that as a kid I thought it a riot when my father would imitate my overweight paternal grandmother grunting and groaning when she exerted herself. Now, when I just bend over to tie a shoe, I hear that same sound, only it isn't coming from my grandmother.

~

I'VE BEEN DISAPPOINTED lately in my decision making. At this stage of my life, for most situations, I should understand the implications, perceive the big picture, before getting involved. Decisions about social activities, where all that's demanded is a little perspicacity and savoir-faire, should be a snap. I had expected to have some of those by now. Regrettably, there is a growing body of evidence to the contrary.

Just one case in point: Recently I took nephew Mark, my ancient Dad and his even more ancient brother Uncle Bob to a Detroit Tigers baseball game. That excursion was the feature attraction of an Oakland University alumni fund-raiser. Thanks to Mark's good navigating, we found the parking lot nearest our gate at Comerica Park, so the trek to the stadium was manageable.

My father loved baseball and was good at it, having played in college and in community leagues. Once, when my dad was in the Army in San Antonio, Frank "Stubby" Overmire, a pitcher and pitching coach for the Detroit Tigers, came to dinner at our house. My father had been one of the few players to get a hit off Stubby at Western State Teachers' College (now Western Michigan University), and the two became friends. Coincidentally, my Dad and Stubby were each born in 1919 and both were about five feet, seven inches tall.

Until that outing to Comerica Park, Dad hadn't been to a game in years because he had so much trouble walking and seeing. Even so, getting into the park for the pre-game festivities went like clockwork. We had arrived very early and easily found the alums' party room. After we had claimed our T-shirts, popcorn, peanuts and pizza, we settled into lounge chairs on the concourse before heading for our seats. For an hour and a half before game time, we watched a steady file of eleven hundred OUers shuffle along the same sequence we had knocked off in mere minutes.

I admit to feeling rather smug we had planned so well— that is, until we began the trek to our seats. What I hadn't considered was our seat location—upper box seats in the third deck. With each increasingly arduous step, I recalled an image from the film, *A Stairway to Heaven,* with that infinitely long flight of steps disappearing into the clouds. As hundreds of fans waited on the stairway behind us, I inched upwards with my two octogenarians, one virtually blind and barely ambulatory, the other bent over as though perpetually stooping to pick something up.

The trip back down proved to be even worse, and worse still was getting back to the car. Dad, sharing his perpetual grin, and Uncle Bob, shuffling forward face down, were stoic. But for them it must have seemed like a descent from Everest, only to be followed by a marathon.

What was at fault here was the original decision. Any clear-thinking adult would have secured lower-level box seats, dropped off the gents at the gate, parked, and had Dad taken to his seat in a wheel chair.

More's the pity. Far from being the exception, what we have here is an all-too-common failure of prudent decision-making.

⁓

MY FATHER WAS a gentleman, almost unfailingly kind, and had good control over his temper. I only saw him lose it twice. Once was when he was replacing firebricks in our fireplace. The problem was, the original bricks had fallen from the area that slanted outward, directing heat into the room. It was like laying bricks on a ceiling. My dad would trowel on some mortar, then place a brick, and splot, the mortar would fall out. He'd redo it and, klunk, a brick would fall out. After an hour of this, the air turned blue with words I'd never heard him use.

The second time was during an extended visit by my mom's mother, a German woman who was used to running her own household. To say my grandmother was high-strung and shrill would be an understatement. My saintly mother just rolled with Grandma's constant advice and criticism. But this visit was protracted, and my father was at home on the weekend when my grandmother stormed out the bathroom declaring that the toilet paper was hanging over the wrong side of the roll, and that in any well-run household, on and on. In a stentorian voice Dad told Grandma that this was our house, our toilet paper roll, and we'd have it our way. It was the first time I'd ever seen my grandmother cowed.

I thought of that incident years later when I learned there was indeed rationale for which way the toilet paper should hang: The proper orientation is indeed over the top, toward the user. I came to know this because my advertising agency had several major clients in sanitary supply, and in my office we had shelves full of trade publications with titles like Commercial Housekeeper and American Innkeeper. These experts took such issues seriously, and so did our client. Imagine serious articles for the hotel manager on the sole topic of how the up-to-snuff housekeeper must fold the exposed end sheet of the toilet paper roll into a point and rest it on the very top of the roll, just so.

Since Dad's long-ago blow-up with Grandma, I have encountered this dilemma in businesses and even, God help me, in some private homes. Perhaps it says something about my lack of self-control, but invariably I compulsively correct that toilet paper mis-orientation. It's a curse.

⌐

BARBARA AND I enjoyed nephew Christopher's and grand niece Colette's stay at the farm during the week-end festivities in honor of son Jason's visit. For all her five years, Colette is a treasure—inquisitive, perceptive, articulate, well-mannered, and sociable with adults and other kids. As if that weren't enough, she's adorable. and a credit to Maryanne's and Christopher's parental love and child-rearing skills. Christopher is good company, too. He's so well-read, it's great talking with him. I find him simpatico because, like me, he's a real word guy. And that's just what exacerbates the one tiny source of irritation during their whole visit.

Being a Francophone, I love the name Colette. I love to say it, love to hear it. The *nom-de-plume* of a much beloved French author, few proper nouns better evoke la belle France. Unfortunately, Christopher calls my grand niece Colettey. Can you believe it? Colettey! Fingernails on a blackboard. My spirit, my very soul rebels. But I'm trying to deal with it. I tell myself that, in my indignation, I'm yielding to the same French cultural and linguistic snobbery I find so irritating in others, and which I'm sure has contributed to *la belle langue* being supplanted by English as the premier international language. Of course I know that the child is oblivious to all this.

I haven't broached the subject with Christopher. What would I say? That, being a dropout French teacher, I find the name Colettey retrograde to civilized discourse? That it reminds me of Americans in France shouting things like, "Look at this purse, Fred. It's like Mildred's but I hate the color. And the *price ...!* " Okay, so maybe I'm just a trifle persnickety about these things, but I find the issue too emotional for polite discussion.

Maybe the solution lies in an intervention, where, as I understand it, typically a group of the offending party's relatives or friends, attempts to change the person's delusional beliefs or objectionable behavior by confronting him or her with the "truth." But who would join me? Who else cares? Besides, it seems unmanly, like I don't have the moxie to handle it myself.

Another possibility. I could try to come to terms with the

situation through discussions with an e-audience on the blog I'm going to launch any day now, the one with the working title "I'm Not Aging Well." An example: Although deep in the study of spirituality born of a combined Buddhist/Christian philosophy and religion, I can still find myself seduced by its antithesis—revenge.

I could reveal in my blog that Christopher has confided in me that he has always been jealous over his brother Scott's being called Scotty; that all his life he has longed to be addressed as Christo-furry. So would you all please call him that? At least as long as he's calling Collette ... I've made my point. Those who say revenge ain't sweet, ain't tasted it.

～

By now, the reader may have sensed that my co-authors and I feel that perhaps we were drawn by some inexplicable power to our wouldn't-miss-it Monday morning coffee and delectable baked treasures at Brioni's. I see that, compared with them, I jumped ahead a few decades without writing much about where I come from. Literally, geographically, that would be Rochester, Michigan, but as I acknowledged earlier, I rejected the town when I lived there, a place of ultra conformity, and have no desire to reminisce.

Well, except about the town dump. That I can wax nostalgic about.

I very much liked going to the dump in Rochester in the days before we had landfills. Today's landfills are the disposal equivalent of big box stores, and you can't even get in them except through a guarded gate and by paying a hefty toll. But in those bygone days, our dump had its charm. A river ran through it and I'd toss bottles in it and shoot them with the single-shot .22 caliber rifle my father bought with money he'd saved by chopping wood. Really what I wanted to do was shoot rats, but I never saw any. At any rate, I shot expert when I was in the Army, and plinking those moving bottles is why. These days shooting a .22 in a landfill would probably get you thrown in the slammer.

In a junior high school art class, I was assigned to compose a framed mosaic wall-hanging out of glass and ceramic shards. These I found in the dump, and recall my joy when I spotted a cobalt blue Bromo Seltzer bottle. The mosaic (a Roman soldier with spear and shield) turned out well. Except that, because one had to compose the design backwards—the shards were placed face down in a frame that was then filled with plaster of Paris—our hero was listing a bit to his military left.

Where I'm coming from in a deeper sense is something else. I've been writing poems since I was seventeen. Because I've never established a writing regimen, my poems happen irregularly, through inspiration. I recently completed the conversion of my dairy barn's milk house into a writer's re-treat, hoping that it will inspire me to compose on a schedule.

So until now, my poems just happened to happen, and al-most always in unpredictable ways, like one I wrote when my wife, Barbara, and I and another couple vacationed in Mexico. We went to a little seaside town an hour north of Puerto Val-larta called La Peita de Jaltemba, or La Peita for short. There we stayed at a lovely inn high on a rock promontory right on the water, with a magnificent view. Right next to the inn and behind the sandy beach was a graveyard that was being washed out to sea, having taken a hit from a recent hurricane.

It was New Year's Eve and we had been invited to a bash in town for expats and prominent citizens. As we walked to the party and eventually back, a bit tipsy, to our B & B, the wind picked up and the waves crashed on the beach. There was a full moon. I went to bed and listened to a loud booming. The image that instantly flashed was that one of the loose, concrete sarcophagi had been hurled against the rock. If you can't make a poem out of this stuff, I maintain, you'd better get out of the business. And so I wrote that poem and it was published in 2006 in the Oakland University literary magazine, and I offer it again here:

La Fiesta:
La Peñita De Jaltemba, Mexico
New Year's Eve 2006

Two hours in amid the lights
Beside the three deep bar
Pozole tamales rice and flan
Still fill the *mesas*

Spent replete in need of sleep
We quit the party early
Retire to our b and b
High upon the basaltic bluff

This year's last full moon
Strews sintered silver
From bay shore below
Far as the world's edge

Beside us to the south
Behind the beach
The sea is swallowing a graveyard
Now half consumed

Some white sarcophagi and crosses
And statues of the Holy Mother
And Christ and plastic flowers
In red yellow and blue remain

While bayside graves the hurricane exposed
Brick and concrete tetrahedrons
Lie like boats aground
Derelict and atilt

Tonight from gusts
And seasonal high tides
Hungry waves lick the tombs
Tile shards and rosaries on the sand

Rocks crack and boom on crypts
Admonishing the guests: Sra. Gomez and
Garcias, Frias, Venturas and Cortez
Recuerdo de sus padres y hermanos

Crack no sleep this nuevo año
Boom come out rejoin the feast
¡Pruebe! like the living
You could try perhaps the crabs

⟿

TIME TO GET myself into my milk house/writer's retreat. Time to immerse myself into one or more of the eight major writing projects stacked up like planes over an airport, waiting to land. Time to get back to them. Time past time to hop-scotch through the days and places of my life, as I did to mine these pages. Yes, to milk a story or two in that old milk house— that's where I'm going from here.

8

FROM KICKIN' CANS IN THE CITY TO CLARKSTON & CONSERVANCY

by Jim Reed

"Men who took part in that strike talked about it for years as a badge of honor, especially an event called 'The Battle of the Bulls Run'."

WHEN I WAS growing up in Flint, Michigan, it was well known as a "GM factory town." There was a good reason for that because we had many General Motors plants: Chevrolet, Buick, AC Spark Plug Division, Ternstedt Tool & Die Division, GM Parts, and Fisher Body.

The population of Flint in the 1930-50s was about 150,000, or half again larger than it is today. When General Motors all but abandoned the city decades later, population declined steadily to under one hundred thousand, the biggest decline ever for any American city of about that size.

During my school days in Flint, it had a bustling downtown centered around Saginaw Street. There was a good public bus system and we could ride for a dime including transfers. The neighborhoods were mixed, as far as the kind of houses went. The older ones near town had what we called shotgun homes—a house with a long hall that ran from the front door straight to the back door. The name came from the claim that you could shoot a gun down the hall from the front door right out the back door and not hit a thing. The houses in the newer areas of the city had small two-bedroom bungalows scattered among older two-story houses.

Every neighborhood had a local store that we could walk to and get groceries, milk, bread, and whatever a parent put on a shopping list. I used to buy five-cent candy at the little store near our house, and Dixie Cups with movie star pictures on the lids.

The city was very segregated and everybody was aware of that from our earliest days. I met my first black kids when we went to a public swimming pool several miles from home. To get to that pool, we had to walk across railroad tracks and cross over Saginaw Street, the main thoroughfare in Flint. In the early 1940s, we'd had a major influx of white southern folks, mainly from Missouri and Arkansas. They had come to our area because Flint's GM Plants were hiring for the war effort. When they first began showing up, it caused some friction for a couple reasons. For one thing, we didn't take to their drawl, and then there was their idea that the "South Will Rise Again." Right away that triggered more than one fight but before long we became friends, mostly due to common school attendance.

Years earlier, my folks had moved to Michigan from the very small town of Big Falls in Koochiching County in Northern Minnesota. The population in Big Falls never got much over five hundred and was usually about half that. My grandpa Reed was the stationary engineer in the saw mill and worked nights. My dad grew up there, hunting with Grandpa and they spent a lot of time in the woods. Grandpa had one arm cut off just above the elbow but he still managed to bring down a lot of game. A major source of income for them was "shining" deer at night and then selling them to the deer hunters who came up from the big cities in southern Minnesota and didn't want to go home empty-handed.

When my dad was a young man, he worked in the logging industry. When they logged large tracts of pine west of town in the winter, he drove four-horse teams. They would drag the logs out of the woods to rail sidings for shipping to the mills or landings on the Big Fork River for the spring log drives. There were several logging camps surrounding Big Falls. My mom talked about visiting the camps on Sundays where all were welcome and could expect a big feed.

Another event Dad often talked about was being on the last log drive on the Big Fork River in the early '20s—to my young ears, that sounded like a real adventure. The logs were dumped into the river at sites called landings and then were convoyed downstream to the Rainy River sawmills and paper mills. The "river hogs" were responsible for keeping the logs moving downstream and sometimes they had to blow log jams with dynamite. The drive was organized around a barge called the "Wanigan" which had bunks and a cook shack. The cook was in charge of the Wanigan and was a key figure, as a poor cook would cost the drive boss many of his crew. Some of these cooks were renowned for their sourdough bread, biscuits, and pancakes and each cook had his own special secret dough. Many of the cooks also spent the winters cooking in the logging camps.

Mom grew up in the same small town and went to State Teachers College in Bemidji where she got a two-year degree. In what must have been a real adventure at the time, she and her sister bought a new car and drove to Montana and got teaching jobs in one-room schools in neighboring towns. She would tell us kids harrowing stories of bitter winters, walking to schools through deep snow, and having to start the wood stove for heat. For two years or so, they boarded with local farm families and stayed in touch with those folks for years.

My mother's family was hard put for funds as their dad died early and left them in tough straits—they had owned the local hotel and a small restaurant but lost all after father's death. Mom and her two sisters took turns working in restaurants while one of the girls went to the teachers' college.

Other than logging and the sawmills, there was very little work in Big Falls. Their brother, my uncle Emerson, worked in the woods, and later became a small-time logger with a sawmill and also ran a farm. My memory of him was of a tall strong silent type who also ran a small bar in town. He was known for running a no-limit poker game on Saturday nights. When I was a small boy I was the bartender at some of those Saturday night poker games. One time I looked down behind the bar and saw what was called a "Saturday night special," a small pistol that I guessed they had stashed there in case someone tried to stage a robbery. We still have that pistol in the family. Even though the rest of the family moved away, Emerson spent his entire life in Big Falls caring for his widowed mother.

In the late '20s, my dad followed his brother to Flint from Minnesota, as GM was hiring lots of folks. He hired into Fisher Body No. 1 along with his brother. A few years later their parents moved to Flint as well. The grandparents bought a house in South Flint and took in boarders because Grandpa could no longer work after having lost an arm in a sawmill accident while in Minnesota. During those years Dad made several trips back to Minnesota and that may have been how he either met or was courting my mother.

When the Great Depression hit in 1933, things got very tough in Flint. Plants dropped lots of workers and those that remained only got a few hours' work per week. I remember many sad tales of those times and you had to wonder how my family and many other families in the same straits got by. My Grandpa lost all his money in a bank failure and would never use banks again; he kept his money in an old tobacco can in a closet. My mom recalled going to the County for food and whatever other assistance could be had. That made Grandpa furious but my mother claimed she needed milk for the baby, which at the time was me.

From 1935 to 1937, everything changed for Flint, for the U.S. automobile industry and for workers nationwide. In 1935, led by Walter Reuther, the UAW was formed and in 1936 held its first convention. The union knew if it was to succeed in organizing the entire domestic automobile industry it had to go after its biggest employer. That decision changed life for everybody in and around Flint because the target chosen by Reuther and the UAW was GM's Flint production complex. The 1937 GM "Sit-Down Strike" brought major changes not only to Flint but also to the rest of the blue-collar workers in the country. As the turning point in the nation in collective bargaining, it was a life-changing event for our family and countless families everywhere. The union fought for and won better wages and working conditions in the plants—everyone benefited from that.

During the strike, folks brought food and drink to the strikers—they had to pass it through windows to get it into the hands of the men holding out inside the plant who were sitting down on the job, refusing to work until their demands for better wages and working conditions were met.

In the middle of January, police tried to enter the plant, brandishing guns and using tear gas, but the workers rebuffed them. After more than two dozen police and workers were injured, and thirteen strikers suffered gunshot wounds, Governor Frank Murphy took steps that made him a local hero. Flint's government and GM pleaded with Murphy to send in the National Guard and he did so, but he ignored a court order directing him to expel the workers. Instead he instructed the Guard to maintain the peace and leave the strikers alone, which was not at all what was expected by city government and GM when they asked the governor to intervene.

Men who took part in that strike talked about it for years as a badge of honor, especially an event called "The Battle of the Bulls Run" where strikers drove the cops away by throwing car door hinges at them. The major player for the United Auto Workers in those tense days was Walter Reuther. He went on to become the President of the UAW and a leader in national efforts for workers. Lots of local businesses and organizations got behind the Flint auto workers in their struggles. A local grocery chain, Hamady Bros., gave the strikers food on credit—for many years thereafter those workers and their families remained loyal to Hamady's. It was well into the '50s before the large chains like Kroger could get into the Flint area. I got my first job as a stock boy at a Hamady store.

At the time, in the late '30s, I knew what was happening in Flint made a big difference to families like mine; I didn't know until later how it had shaped national labor policy for decades to come.

⁓

EVEN AS YOUNG kids, we were aware of things like the Depression, men being out of work, and important things happening at the GM plant, but we also knew there was school to go to and games to play, lots of games that you could do for free. We entertained ourselves with scrub baseball games where the kids who owned the ball or bat would be captain and get to choose up sides. We built our own ball field in a vacant lot—I had no idea who owned it. We would make a backstop good enough to keep the ball from rolling too far away when the catcher missed it. We made bases out of whatever was handy and used the family's lawn mowers to cut the grass.

That's what we'd do in the heat of the day and in the evening we'd play Kick the Can, Pom Pom Pull-away, Tag, Mumbly Peg and Enny Anny-Over. We built camps underground in vacant fields and had our first smokes in them (Wings cigarettes at ten cents a pack).

All of us kids followed the Tigers and our local high school teams. After dinner, we would listen to radio programs like *Jack Armstrong, Green Hornet,* and *The Lone Ranger.* The highlight of the week was the Saturday matinee at the local movie theatre. For a dime admission, we would sit through a main feature (usually a cowboy show), news reels, cartoons, previews of coming attractions, and the ongoing serial episode of *Flash Gordon, The Perils of Pauline, Tarzan,* and other heroes. If there was a double feature, we'd be in the theatre all afternoon.

We did some roller skating with clamp-on skates, and played other games on the sidewalks like hop-scotch. On hot summer days we had a continual Monopoly game going with no limit on borrowing from the bank. On rare occasions we'd go on a picnic to a local County park that had been built by the Civilian Conservation Corps in the early days of the Great Depression. All the boys had BB guns and were always trying to shoot sparrows—for some reason, we thought there was a one cent bounty on them, but I don't think anyone ever got one. We also had BB gun wars in vacant fields and it is a wonder no one got a serious injury. In the winter we built snow forts, had snowball fights and played hockey on a neighbor's side lot which they flooded for us. Of course we had no nets, goals or boards, so we just used a pair of boots for the goal.

For the kids who had enough enthusiasm, or need, there were always small odd jobs where you could make a little money. In the winter, I would go door to door to line up snow-shoveling jobs; in the summer there were chores like cutting lawns. Every once in a while we would have big paper drives where we were able to get a penny a pound and that seemed like Big Money to me. Daily paper route jobs were hard to come by but eventually I was able to get one.

Compared with living in the country, my schools were nearby and so I walked to both grade school and junior high, whether it was rain, or windy, or snowing. It was only about five blocks to elementary school but close to a mile for junior high. That meant I could walk home for lunch when I was in grade school and while I ate lunch I could listen with my Mom to the soap operas on the radio. In grade school, we got a small bottle of milk every day that I think we paid about two cents for. In junior high, most of us brown-bagged it due to cost of lunch at the cafeteria.

No matter what grade we were in, every day we did the Pledge of Allegiance.

When I got to junior and senior high school, the big event of the week was the school dance and in season it was the football game after school on Fridays. In junior high if a guy got rowdy in class the male teacher would take us out to the hall and hit us with a big paddle board with holes in it; I can state for a fact that really did sting. Although we had large class sizes, we actually had few discipline problems. We all knew if we got in trouble at school and our folks found out we'd be in even bigger trouble at home. If the lady teachers needed to discipline a boy they sent him to the shop teacher who used his paddle. No one thought anything of this punishment. For whatever reason, I don't remember that the girls had any discipline problems.

Very few of us had a license or access to the family car, so we did a lot of walking and hung out at the local stores drinking Cokes and playing the pin ball machines. A big date night was to walk your girl to the bus stop and go downtown to see a movie. We always had to meet the parents as well.

After I started high school at Flint Tech, we had great times just hanging out, cruising through the drive-in burger places. We spent memorable hours at drive-in movie theaters aptly nick-named "passion pits." Groups of guys and gals went everywhere and just enjoyed the mobility of cars, summer days, school events and of course the Saturday night movies, our standard date night. Years later, I observed that the movie *American Graffiti* captured very well the feel and sense of that time of life, the Fifties in America.

My high school, Flint Tech, had excellent math and science teachers and we got a solid engineering grounding there. I got a very sound education in the Flint schools and had some dedicated teachers. My eighth-grade English teacher, Mr. Bacon, taught me all that I needed to do well in high school and college.

I was in grade school when the Japanese bombed Pearl Harbor but it seemed to me then that only my dad knew where Pearl Harbor was. Those World War II years were certainly a scary time for all. The neighborhood Air Raid Wardens walked around with their white hats and told everybody to shut off the lights. Dad and all men in our areas worked six and seven days a week and even some mothers got jobs in lighter work in support of the war effort. Dad's job at Fisher Body was machining military tank turrets. I always expected Dad to get drafted but due to his responsibilities for the family and his job, that didn't happen.

With the war, everything changed again. Ration books and coupons were required for just about everything—gas, food, shoes, sugar, clothes. I later learned there was a "black market" and that was how some of the most scarce rationed items could be gotten. I knew little about that but heard that some farmers had lots of gasoline they would sell for the right price. We got all our news from local newspaper and broadcasts on the radio, but looking back on it now, it was often loaded with propaganda. I remember there was intense hatred of the Japanese, but not so much of the Germans. When we played soldiers no one wanted to be the Japs.

The end of WWII brought good times. My dad got a foreman's job and so my folks got a new Buick. We were doing well as were most of our neighbors. We even went on a few trips to northern Minnesota to visit my parents' home town. We took lovely drives through the Upper Peninsula along Lakes Michigan and Superior. Having lived in Flint during my childhood, my only taste of small town life was in Big Falls. There I swam in the river, played ball, and competed in the Fourth of July events. The town even had its own parade and celebration events. Everyone in that town knew everyone else and I heard many stories about how it was growing up there. The treasured memories and friendships of small town life in America are a way of life that is disappearing.

~~

I REMEMBER THOSE days as really great times. None of us had any real plans for the future and before graduation many young couples were talking marriage, which for some reason seemed so important to us. Jobs were easy to get in the GM plants and paid good money, so many went directly from high school into the plants. At that time, you expected, if you hired into GM, you had a guaranteed job for life. I went to GMI (General Motors Institute of Technology; now known as Kettering University) as an engineering co-op from a Fisher plant and stayed through my fifth-year program and graduated in 1956.

In 1953, I married my high school sweetheart, Barb. We bought our first home soon thereafter in Flint for ten thousand dollars. Our first son, Jon, was born in 1955 and, after GMI, I transferred to Fisher Body General Offices and we moved there (in Warren) in 1957. I stayed with GM until 1987, moving to the Tech Center and into executive jobs.

After leaving GM, I went into consulting (primarily on Lean Manufacturing concepts) and worked in Ann Arbor at the National Center for Manufacturing Sciences. We had three more sons and a nice life in Warren with lots of boating, camping and driving vacations. Later there were wilderness canoe trips in northern Ontario with white water, rough water, tough portages and indelible memories. We discovered water skiing soon after acquiring our boat and all our kids got very proficient in that sport. We were still skiing into the '90s although I've since quit. We still have our original boat from the '60s which our sons maintain as a family tradition.

I did many "fly-in" fishing trips to remote camps in Ontario with family and friends, as well as deer and pheasant hunting. My sons and I spent many November days in deer camp in the Pigeon River Country Forest. We would pitch a large tent and the boys would build a sort of lean-to for cooking. Sometimes we would just spend several days chasing around the woods. Those were experiences none of the family have every forgotten, and we even got a few deer in Pigeon River country, some of the nicest undeveloped land in the Lower Peninsula. In those tranquil remote areas, miles from any road, the only sound is the murmur of the river and the call of the loons.

ᴐ

In 1981, to get away from congestion and traffic, we moved to Clarkston and have been here since. Finally, in 1994 I retired and increased my involvement in a local land conservancy by which I helped save some of our pristine natural areas.

As the crow flies, it is not many miles from Flint to Clarkston. But along the way, there have been some interesting stops and countless indelible memories.

9

CHRIS READING'S TIPS FOR SUCCESS IN TENNIS... AND IN LIFE

*"He helped the downtrodden through his politics
and policy support, and with his hands-on initiative."*
—Bob McGowan

CHRIS READING WAS an early member of the group that for
several years has gathered Monday mornings for coffee
at Brioni Cafe & Deli in Clarkston. Chris added a unique point
of view as we solved the problems of the world only to have to
do it all over again the next week.

Everybody around the table brought something special. In
many ways, though, Chris's contributions were extra special.
For one thing, he was the only Kiwi in the bunch, having traveled half way around the globe from New Zealand on his own
personal road less traveled to arrive finally at Clarkston.

A good measure of esteem for a friend is how much you
want to spend time with him or her. I, like so many of Chris'
other friends, always wanted to hang out, talk, and do projects with him. Chris had enormous generosity of spirit, giving
freely and profusely of his time and talent. Whether it was
repairing his friends' mechanical equipment, aiding in their

home improvement, working in their gardens, mentoring students, raising funds for organizations through woodworking projects, and much more, Chris was always there.

His compassion for others was not confined to his friends. He helped the disadvantaged and the downtrodden through his politics and policy support, and with his hands-on initiative.

A citizen of both the United States and New Zealand, his dual nationality gave him a keen political and sociological perspective, a sort of binocular vision that allowed him to consider issues in their breadth and depth.

Chris was enormously vital. In tennis, bicycling, gardening, he was energetic and positive. His energy was infective. You felt energized when you were with him. He did everything with good humor, sometimes critically, but was never unfair or unkind. Chris had a keen wit, when speaking or writing, and loved to laugh. And he had a rich sense of the absurd.

Always the engineer, the profession from which he retired, he saw problems as things to be solved. He was developing a low-cost world truck for assembly and sale in third-world countries, which would help raise people out of poverty. That program has at least been put on hold.

Among so many of his other skills, Chris was a fine gardener and an expert composter. His compost bins looked like illustrations in a gardening magazine. Chris would walk into the garden, look around, and identify the things that most needed to be done, and, often, tasks that he could do best.

His greatest legacy is, of course, his family—his wife Gail, their four sons, and their families. They were always first in his consciousness and in his heart. It would delight Chris no end that Gail occasionally brings her point of view and her smile to the Monday morning coffee group at Brioni Cafe & Deli.

Chris Reading was a sharp-eyed student of sports, as

well as of human nature. His treatise, "Essentially Tennis," focuses on how to achieve full potential at tennis. But it does much more than that—it offers lessons for how to succeed on any project, or how to attack any problem. And even how to live a life.

A young person embarking on that first position in an organization, an entrepreneur launching that initial venture would do well to keep Chris' techniques for cultivating a winning attitude prominently pasted at eye level. A person of any age will find guidance in developing a fresh outlook to deal with the everyday challenges of life. Here are excerpts from Chris' "Essentially Tennis" treatise:

> **HAVE FUN**. If you aren't having fun, you're missing out.

> **PLAY TO WIN.** It's your best incentive for superior tennis performance.

> **KEEP SCORE.**

> **CONCENTRATE.** Focus exclusively on the ball, the match, the court, and your opponent.

> **BE CONFIDENT.** Recall that recently you have executed each stroke well. Know that you can do it again. It's rather a matter of **REPEAT PERFORMANCE** than of **DISCOVERY.**

> **MINIMIZE YOUR ERRORS.** Keep that ball in play, but **DON'T BE INHIBITED** or overly cautious. **GO** for those **WINNERS** when they present themselves.

STAY COOL. Exhibit **RESOLUTION** and **DETERMINATION** and a sense of knowing what is happening. **BE THERE.**

CAPITALIZE on your strengths and **EXPLOIT** your opponent's weaknesses.

Keep your opponent on the **DEFENSIVE.** Hit into the open court, or where he/she **LEAST EXPECTS** you to hit.

Don't play to a **PREDICTABLE PATTERN** unless it's a winning strategy.

Always **CHANGE A LOSING GAME.** Exercise all your options in your search for a winning strategy.

Stay **LOOSE.** Relaxed, yet alert. Physically and mentally.

PREPARE EARLY.

Hit with **AUTHORITY.**

ASSERT your influence and ensure your **FOLLOW-THROUGH.**

Last, but not least, **STUDY HARD, PRACTICE HARD, PLAY HARD...**and **BE HOME BY TEN.**

⌒

CHRIS READING WAS *born in Auckland, New Zealand, and be-came a teenage regional tennis champion. After a four-year engineering degree, he was selected by General Motors to do a two-year post graduate study at GMI in Flint, Michigan. He was a member of the Institute of Production Engineers of Great Britain. In the words of Gail Reading, "Chris was many things to many people, including a tinkerer, a dreamer, and a visionary who lived his life trying to make the world a better place."*

The Clarkston Coffee compatriots, gathering Monday mornings at Brioni's, raise a glass of New Zealand wine to toast Chris for good times and lessons learned.

≈ 10 ≈

Mining Memories on the Mesa, the Mediterranean and Manistique
by Floyd "Buck" Kopietz

"It is important to have dreams—the only thing worse than an unfulfilled dream is to have no dream at all."

M Y STORY BEGINS in the same town in Michigan's Upper Peninsula that also gave birth a hundred years ago to Paul Bunyan, at least that is the myth in Manistique. Yes, I am a Yooper. Although I am known as "Buck" Kopietz, I began life named Floyd Clifford after my grandfather on my mother's side. Both my dad and mom were children of the Great Depression, growing up in the Detroit area. My mom's family lived in Royal Oak and my dad's family on the east side of Detroit.

When World War II broke out, my dad joined the Army and spent four years in England, seeing combat action in the invasions of North Africa, Sicily and Italy. He met my mom ten months before the end of the War while he was on leave and they married before he went back on duty.

When Dad was discharged in 1945 he benefited from the

Mustering-out Payment Act of 1944. This gave each service-man enough money to help start a new life after the War. Dad and Mom decided to buy a resort in the U.P. on a small lake about twelve miles north of Manistique, Michigan. Dad loved hunting and Mom was a really good sport. This is where I was born. Manistique's claim to fame was a very large sign in the shape of a lumberman that said Paul Bunyan was born there a hundred years ago. I always enjoyed knowing I was born in the same town as the famous Paul Bunyan.

The resort my parents purchased was primitive, actually very primitive. None of the log cabins—including our home—had indoor plumbing or electricity.

I am guessing they bought the resort in the spring of 1946 because they always talked about some of the things they did that would not have been possible after I came along. They often would fondly tell the stories about hunting ducks with a .22. Evidently Mom was something of an Annie Oakley—she could shoot ducks on the fly with that .22. They collected maple sap during their first spring and made maple syrup on the wood stove. They only did this once and I learned early that it takes a lot of sap to make a little syrup.

The first hunting season my dad went out early in the morning and bagged his deer quickly. He then spent the rest of the hunting season helping the rest of the hunters in get-ting their deer.

I came along on October 2, 1947, just before opening day of their second hunting season at the resort. I was named af-ter my Grandfather Floyd Clifford Ferguson on my mom's side. Running a hunting camp, especially as primitive as this one, had to have been a lot of work. Because of me, Dad was not able to hunt that season as Mom needed the extra help. The hunters that year were very understanding telling Dad not to worry because he already got his buck. The hunters began calling me Buck and the name stuck.

Running a primitive resort in the Upper Peninsula of Michigan with only a three-month summer season and a short hunting season was not a financial winner for my parents. Dad had to find extra work for the off season, coming down to Detroit and staying with Grandpa Kopietz. I am fairly certain Mom and I came with him.

During my second winter with my parents in Detroit, the previous owner of the resort filed a lawsuit against my parents. My parents hired a lawyer in Manistique to handle the case. Right idea, wrong choice of lawyer—they ended up losing everything except me. Well, not quite everything. Fortunately, they had sold one of the cabins to Mom's parents the previous year. That cabin—outhouse and all—stayed in the family for over twenty-eight years and that was where I spent nearly all of my summers growing up. We did eventually get electricity, but not indoor plumbing.

﹏

AFTER LOSING THE resort, Dad took a training job with Excello Corporation in Highland Park, so we became permanent residents in Eastside Detroit with my Grandpa Kopietz on Bewick Street. That is where my childhood memories began. The house was a two-story brick with stairs on the front going up to a covered stoop and the front door. The rooms seemed small, even to me at three years of age. There was a back door with steps going down to a very small back yard.

It is here that I learned my first lesson: Do not pull your pants down before you get to the bathroom to save time. You might trip and lose your front teeth hitting the toilet with your face. I am not sure how many years I went without front teeth but it was a long time. It gave me my theme song for most of my early youth, the recording by Spike Jones and his City

Slickers, *All I Want for Christmas is My Two Front Teeth*. Even after my new teeth finally grew in, everyone would sing that song for me at Christmas time.

My Grandpa Kopietz became my best friend. He was retired so we spent a lot of time together watching television and taking walks. We watched *Hopalong Cassidy* together as he really enjoyed westerns. In 1950 and '51, when I was three and four years old, we took walks, usually to the corner beer garden. People there were really friendly and Grandpa enjoyed showing me off. I must have been a '50s Rockwell picture with my red hair, freckles. and two missing front teeth. I had fun playing table shuffleboard, just whizzing the pucks down the board. To this day when I go into a real bar, that special beer smell brings back fond memories of Grandpa and our time together. This is also where I developed a taste for pickled hard-boiled eggs and pickled sausage. My Grandfather and best friend passed away in August of 1952 just before I turned five.

⁓

DAD HAD BEEN training at Excello Corp in their Pure Pak Division to be a service engineer. Pure Pak had been purchased by Excello in the 1940's and began manufacturing the machines to package milk in wax-coated paper cartons. All milk before this came in glass bottles. The company was going to be installing machines in dairies throughout the South during the fall of 1952 and Dad would be part of the workforce doing those installations. Mom and I came along with him. We drove through the Smoky Mountains and I was in awe. For the first time I took notice of landscapes. We stayed in boarding houses and what today would be called Bed & Breakfasts although I am not sure they served breakfasts.

We stayed for what must have been weeks in both Savannah and Charleston, the only two cities my parents ever mentioned when talking about this trip later in my life. These were probably the only two places we stayed close to the ocean. It was probably Charleston where we stayed in a boarding house. It was here I met my first friend other than family. He was a grownup and worked at the boarding house. He spent time with me, telling me stories and must have made a good impression on me because he was the only person other than my parents that I remember from that trip. He also happened to be of dark skin. All the people in my life up to that time were of light skin.

In Charleston, Dad took me to a pier for fishing for the first time. We caught ocean perch, although I did not remember actually catching the fish but I do remember the fish bleeding. My poor dad who loved hunting and fishing was forced to let the fish go. He must have been devastated. I am sure he looked forward to having a son who would enjoy hunting with him someday and his five-year-old son cannot even fish because he might be hurting the fish. While I never could shoot a deer or bird, I did grow to enjoy fishing.

The boarding house was close to the water, with waves breaking on the beach. Growing up in Michigan I was used to the Great Lakes but there was something very different about the ocean. The smell of the ocean, the breakers, the wide beaches, and the shells strewn over them was pretty cool for a little kid.

My mom and I flew back to Michigan for Christmas so we could be with my Grandpa and Grandma Ferguson in Royal Oak. Flying was a new experience for many people at that time. While I don't remember that experience myself, Mom must have not enjoyed it because she never liked flying after that trip.

That Christmas my mom took me to see Santa Claus at

Hudson's in downtown Detroit. One whole floor was devoted entirely to Christmas. To me it felt like I was at the North Pole, the same feeling countless adults recall fondly when talking about a trip to Hudson's during Christmas when they were young.

A storm had dumped considerable snow during the holidays that year. My Aunt Kay, Uncle Dave and cousins, Bonnie and Butch, came for Christmas dinner. My cousins brought their new skis, so Uncle Dave piled snow high enough to make a five-foot ski ramp and we skied after dinner. My Uncle Fred—who was only eleven years older than me—got a BB pistol and a target that had spinning figures that would spin when they were hit with the BB. I got to shoot at the target although I am not sure I hit anything.

We were now living with Mom's parents on Lexington in Royal Oak in a bigger house with a big yard that backed up to a public woods. It was a two-story arts-and-crafts home with white asbestos shingles and no back porch. It did have a full basement and a detached garage directly in back of the house. There was a side porch with a milk chute off a large kitchen with a breakfast nook. An opening led to a full dining room with a large dark wood buffet, china cabinet, and large dining room table with heavy chairs with red leather seats and backs. All the wood was heavy and intricately carved. Everyone in the family thought that eventually they would like to have the dining set. Many years later, after my grandparents passed away, no one had a dining room large enough to accommodate the set. My parents ended up with the set but were never able to use it and it ended up being stored.

The living room seemed large and had a television set with a small screen in a dark wood console and a little red light at the bottom of the console that lit up when the TV was on. Grandpa had lots of clocks that he kept in good condition so there was constant ticking and hourly chiming twenty-four hours a day. I became used to the ticking and chime and actually miss it today. There was a light blue sofa and two large upholstered chairs. The one my grandma always sat in was a dark red. There were two end tables with drawers holding many treasures. I would poke through the drawers to see if there was anything new, but I never got tired of looking at the postcards. The ones I liked the most had pictures of totem poles. There was also a Viewmaster with round disks with photos embedded around the perimeter—a little lever advanced from one three-dimensional image to the next. There were photos of totem poles on these disks as well. Many years later I learned that the postcards and 3-D photo disks were sent to my grandparents by Uncle Dave who was in the Coast Guard during World War II and stationed in Juneau, Alaska. I also learned many years later that he drove landing craft during island invasions in the Pacific.

Another treasure in the drawer was a harmonica that belonged to Grandpa Ferguson. He would play it for me every once in awhile. When I was alone in the living room, I would sometimes have fun blowing into it. You don't have to know what you are doing to make something close to music on a harmonica. A few years later while playing with the harmonica, I accidentally played a few bars of *Red River Valley* and I realized with experimenting I could play songs.

⌐

MY GRANDPARENTS OWNED a dry goods store in Royal Oak called Ferguson's Dry Goods. Their first location was on Main Street just north of Second Street. On the corner of Second and Main was a drug store with a soda fountain where you could get the best cherry cokes. On Second just west of Washington Street, in the first floor of the Washington Square Building, was a

Sander's Candy Store. There were swivel chairs facing long marble counters and you could swivel back and forth until they served your lunch. What you really looked forward to for dessert was a bowl with ice cream swimming in the best fudge in the world. Up on the walls a few feet below the ceiling were shelves with plush animals and that is where Grandma got me my first teddy bear.

A block from my grandma's store on Main Street was Hermann's Bakery where my grandparents bought breads that were very different and made especially good toast. I suspect my mother grew up with this bread because any time we were in Michigan, she would go out of her way to get this bread.

⁓

AFTER MY DAD returned from the South, my parents started talking about moving to the Southwest. My dad had become a service engineer and was given a territory in New Mexico servicing the dairies' milk-packaging machines. None of our relatives nor my parents' friends seemed to know much about the Southwest. Some actually thought we were going to a foreign country and a few even thought we may be in danger from Indians. Their only information about the west came from TV shows and westerns. I don't remember how I felt about it but some time during the summer of my fifth year, we moved to Roswell, New Mexico, a location that would become a magnet for people attracted to stories of visits to Earth from extra-terrestrials. While we lived in Roswell there was never any mention of the 1947 UFO crash.

We moved into a small bungalow on a dirt road. Across from our house was a large alfalfa field next to a field with a barbed wire fence to keep in cows and at least one bull. Every once in a while a cow would get out and graze on our lawn. My friend Tommy and I liked making paths in the alfalfa field until the farmer complained to my parents.

We made frequent trips to the nearby El Capitan Mountains, the birthplace of Smokey the Bear who was rescued as a cub after a forest fire. It was an easy day trip. There was a trading post built into the side of a mountain where we went frequently for supplies and my parents bought me a feather headband, bow and arrow and wood-handled rubber hatchet that seemed like the real thing to a six-year-old.

During our year in Roswell we visited White Sands and the amazing Carlsbad Caverns where a long winding path descended into a large hole in the ground. Down in the cave, lights along the pathway cast a glow on the strange formations above us. We walked for a long time and finally the cave opened up into a very big room with tables and a cafeteria. I have been back since and it still is a fascinating experience.

One of the dairies that Dad serviced was in El Paso. Mom and I went with him several times while we were in Roswell and later as well, an added attraction being visits to Juarez across the border in Mexico. We would park on the American side and walk across the bridge over the Rio Grande. There were always "Chiclet Kids" selling Chiclets gum on the Mexican side of the bridge next to the poverty-stricken communities of cardboard and scrap wood houses.

In the tourist areas, street vendors offered jewelry, Mexican jumping beans and other trinkets. All leather products were stamped with designs, mostly with floral patterns. I got a leather belt and my first wallet and Mom always got her purses in Juarez until we eventually moved back to Michigan. The liquor stores were very popular with the tourists. We usually had dinner at a nightclub that played mariachi music, for which I developed a liking.

The next summer we moved to Albuquerque into a small house in a new subdivision on the northeast side of town. It would be a few years before new subdivisions would be built on the open spaces of the mesa behind us. Dad built a screened-in patio on the back and eventually closed in the back yard with a cement block fence. Several years after moving into our home, the city began building McKinley Junior High directly behind us. I would go there a few years after it was finished. My grade school, Bel Aire, was on the same property but a quarter mile away, closer to more established neighborhoods. There was a path through the field that I would follow to go to school. There were no trees but there was a lot of tumble-weed and vicious goat-head weeds with seeds that looked like a goat's head with horns that I learned were very painful.

I loved going to the drive-in movies that were close to us. Cartoons would be shown before the main feature to make coming to the movies more pleasurable for the kids, most of whom would be asleep in their pajamas during the main feature. My parents took me to many drive-in movies over the years, only a few of which I remember, like *Blood Alley* with John Wayne and Lauren Bacall. A special favorite was *Around the World In 80 Days* with David Niven, Cantinflas and Shirley MacLaine. That movie instilled in me a strong desire to travel, an enthusiasm fed by my parents as they exposed me to many different places and experiences.

Our neighborhood had lots of kids close to my age. Boys and girls often played games together like kick the can, hopscotch, jacks, tetherball, snipe hunts at night, and hide and seek. Nearby Comanche Street was built on a minor arroyo, a depression made by occasional running water. Every time there were strong rains in the Sandia Mountains just to the east, a current of water a few inches deep would build up and soon we would have our makeshift boats racing down the current. We were oblivious that not far away in other arroyos walls of water would cascade down from the Sandias, sometimes washing away car and driver.

The mesa surrounding Albuquerque is considered high desert, affording an environment unlike any other. In the movie *Lawrence of Arabia,* the reporter asks, "What is it, Major Lawrence, that attracts you personally to the desert?" When Lawrence answered, "It's clean," I understood what he meant. Deserts in their natural state are uncomplicated and open. I played with lizards and had a pet horny toad. There were ground squirrels and road runners. I even enjoyed the strong winds that brought sand storms, although that was one reason Mom hated living there. One storm was so strong that we had to scrape off a top layer of sand and then use a canister vacuum cleaner to clean the remainder of the lawn.

My friends and I built round forts into the ground, covered them with scrap wood and adorned them with makeshift decorations. We had earth seats and a makeshift table. It was like a version of a Native American kiva.

When I was about ten or eleven years old, some friends and I hiked some five miles up to the base of Sandia Mountains where we would be gone for most of the day. Our parents didn't seem to have a second thought about our safety then or when we played pickup tackle football without helmets or pads. We did trick or treating at Halloween until 9 or 9:30 without an adult and rode our bicycles for miles to swim at a public pool.

Grade school was fun. Playing marbles was a big thing at recess and lunch time. The way our version of the game was played, the boy running the game would put a line of marbles in front of him. Players would take their shots at the marbles, calling out in advance their target marble and getting to keep the target marble if they hit it. But if they missed, the boy operating the game would get to keep the shooter's marble. It did not take me long to learn that the operator had the advantage. I set myself up as one of the operators—Gambling Lesson No. 1. But then, the school principal came on the scene. He ruled this was not a game of skill but a game of chance, shutting down my growing business.

My second gambling lesson came when when I was about eleven. Dad had taught me to play cribbage and I was fairly good at it. An adult neighbor who was a friend of the family asked if I wanted to play cribbage with him. My parents were in the living room talking with the man's wife. I said, sure. He then asked if I wanted to play for money. I thought I was fairly good and might be able to win—until I lost five or six dollars. My parents were livid when they found out and only later did they discover the neighbor had a major gambling problem.

⁓

IF EVERYONE IS entitled to fifteen minutes of fame, I have only five minutes left because I used up ten in the fifth grade. My fifth-grade teacher decided to teach the class square dancing. She designated me as the square dance caller so I learned quite a few square dances. A classmate, Betty Purvis, had a dad who was a local celebrity because he had a children's after-school TV show called *The Jim Purvis Show* supposedly set at his ranch, although he did not really have a ranch in Albuquerque. He did have local western talent and some nationally known talent on his show, including Glen Campbell who got his start in Albuquerque. In the big moment of my young life, I was up there center stage, lip-syncing the calling of the square dance lyrics as my classmates did their steps. It was the high point in the life of a ten-year-old kid and truly exciting stuff.

Much of the time when I wasn't in class, I was with my two best friends in New Mexico. Charles Dingman was really smart and he and I did neat stuff like making a giant box kite with bamboo poles collected from a carpet store. Back then, new carpets were rolled up on bamboo poles and they always had a stack available. Charles also built a rocket-powered model glider we would fly for long distances in the constant winds above the mesa behind us. When we were in junior high, a small airport was built a few miles to the north of town for small planes and before long flights of real gliders were launched from that airport. Charles and I would fantasize that was going to be our next project, building a real glider—but like most kids' flights of fancy, it never got off the ground. It is important to have dreams—the only thing worse than an unfulfilled dream is to have no dream at all.

Charles and his brother did follow through on a more down-to-earth project—they built a wooden, open car that one person could sit in. The front axle was attached to a flat board that swiveled and your feet would rest on the front axle and that is how you would steer the car. Comanche Road had a serious grade and you could get some real speed going down this road. Amazingly no one died. We thought that car was about as good as it gets. But then, the neighbor kids several doors down built a similar car—except that they added a lawn mower engine to power it.

⁓

MY PARENTS TOOK me on many day trips to see New Mexico's amazing sights and attractions, like Santa Fe, Taos, Farmington, and Gallup. We went to the Jemez Mountains to collect rocks and fossils and often visited Tent Rocks. These geological structures were white conical-shaped soft volcanic rock. We would collect what was known as Apache Tears—actually volcanic glass called obsidian—small clear black pebbles that could be as big as the end of a thumb. We discovered a hollowed-out cave just large enough for several people to get into to get out of the weather. It had smoke stains along the walls and ceiling and you wondered how it must have been for those early people huddled there.

One of our early day trips was to Bandelier National Monument in the Jemez Mountains not too far from Los Alamos. These were Anasazi cliff dwellings similar to Mesa Verde National Park only on a smaller scale. We walked through all the dwellings and could feel how these people must have lived.

New Mexico was a constant learning-by-osmosis experience from which I absorbed a sense of the distinguishing features of different cultures, even though I didn't fully understand that at the time. We visited many Pueblos including Taos, Zuni, Santa Clara, Cochiti, Acoma and Santa Domingo. These strong Hispanic and Native American influences played an important part in my life. Shirley MacLaine once said, "The more I traveled the more I realized that fear makes strangers of people who should be friends." Traveling when I was very young, I never experienced fears and, to the contrary, I developed a lifelong respect for Native American and Hispanic cultures.

On one day trip, we picked up an older gentleman hitchhiker who needed a ride back to his home in the Santa Domingo Pueblo. He told us he had once been the governor of that Pueblo. He invited us into his home, an adobe in the traditional pueblo style with posts used to support the roof which stuck out from the adobe walls. The floor was also adobe rather than wood or tile. There was the traditional outdoor oven which looked like a large adobe cone with a hole in the side where the food, primarily flat bead, could be placed. Another hole at the bottom in the back of the oven is where wood was placed to stoke the fire. I accepted it as second nature that my parents were quickly friendly with people who had been strangers minutes before.

The manager of Creamland Dairy in Gallup and his family became our friends. My dad would regularly service the dairy's milk-packaging machines. The manager's daughter, Cindy, was my age so I had someone to play with whenever we went with my dad. The family lived outside of Gallup near open spaces with large cottonwood trees where we would play with Native American kids. The dairy was close to the Zuni Pueblo and Cindy's parents must have known some of the elders in the Pueblo fairly well because once we were invited to a special Shalako ceremony in an adobe building. I sat on Dad's shoulders so I could watch the very tall costumed men dance.

Not too far south of Santa Fe, off Highway 14 which is known as the Turquoise Trail, is the ghost town of Cerrillos where we explored several deserted buildings and walked into open abandoned mines where we saw interesting rocks. Only years later, when my wife and I owned a jewelry store in Clarkston, Michigan, did I learn that Cerrillos was an ancient historic place, the oldest known mine in North America. Legend tells of the Aztecs mining there over six hundred years ago; perhaps even earlier natives sought the turquoise so prized by many Southwestern tribes.

⌒

EACH YEAR WITHIN a week of my elementary school in New Mexico letting out, my mom would pack me up in our 1956 red Pontiac station wagon and we would head back to Michigan, usually taking Route 66. In June 1955, when I was seven years old, my brother Gary was born, so we postponed our trip to Michigan by several weeks. Mom did not like living in New Mexico and complained about the wind and the lack of lush green vegetation. She also missed her parents back in Michigan even though being with them for any period of time would deteriorate into bad feelings especially with my grandma. Even so, Mom wanted to be home in Michigan and so my brother and I would be packed up after school was out and we would make the trip back to Michigan for the summer, an important influence on my life. Taking different routes, we saw many marvelous sites, like Rocky Mountain National Park. We watched Seven Falls light up with different color lights; visited the Valley of the Gods, Mt. Rushmore, the Bad Lands, Yellowstone, and Old Faithful. All along the way, we kept on the lookout for Burma-Shave signs, carefully spaced along the roadside. Their jingles were amusing and we always tried to memorize them to pass on to our relatives in Michigan.

> *Spring*
> *Is sprung*
> *The grass has riz*
> *Where last year's*
> *Careless drivers is*
> *Burma-Shave*

> *Drinking drivers*
> *Don't you know*
> *Great bangs*
> *From little*
> *Binges grow?*
> *Burma-Shave*

Often the trip was blistering hot and Mom and Grandma tried everything to keep the sweltering car a bit cooler, hanging wet towels over an open window. Oklahoma and Missouri in July were blistering hot and humid and did not cool down much at night. I always could tell when we crossed into Michigan because everything seemed greener and fresher, especially coming through the Irish Hills. That meant soon we would have a Vernor's Ginger Ale Ice Cream Float and New Era Potato Chips out of a large tin with the silhouette of the nude lady on the front.

We usually spent a couple of weeks in the Royal Oak area, staying with my grandparents. I would get to spend a week with my cousins Bonnie and Butch. We would eat lunch while being entertained by the televised *Soupy Sales* show, and in the afternoon by watching *American Bandstand*. My cousins introduced me to popular music.

My aunt and uncle lived in a very small house on the border of Berkley and Royal Oak. My cousins slept in a refinished attic. There was no air conditioning then and it was hot and stuffy sleeping in that room. Aunt Kay was from the Upper Peninsula and like many people with Scandinavian heritage, she gave her kids cod liver oil in the morning, including me when I was visiting there.

Being back in Michigan meant trips north to the cabin. Mackinac Bridge was started in May 1954, so before it opened in November 1957 we would take a whole day driving up to Mackinaw City. Very early on I learned that some words aren't pronounced the way they look. Mackinac is one such word. It is French and it is pronounced like "Mackinaw," with the "c" silent.

On the drive north, it could be boring and so I would watch the road signs to see if we were coming up on a familiar spot: Pinconning, Standish, Grayling, and there was the Call of the Wild Museum and Sea Shell City, just where they were the last time.

We would stay overnight in a motel with cabins along the highway between Cheboygan and Mackinaw City. This would allow us to get up very early to try and catch the first ferry boat across to the U.P. The gulls would make a racket fighting for any food left around. Finally we would hear the blast of horns from the ferry boats. The ferry ride always seemed long but we were able to get out of our cars and go above-decks to look out on Lake Michigan and Lake Huron and I would always wonder where one lake ended and the other began. There was always a breeze and the fresh smell of the lakes that somehow has an aroma like no other.

When Big Mac, the longest expansion bridge in the world at that time, opened in 1957, that ended our ferry trips to the U.P. No longer did we have those very long trips to our cabin on Island Lake. We didn't know it then, but in ten years I-75 would be finished and the whole trip would take only seven hours.

My summers at the cabin were like one long summer camp. The resort was now owned by the Brady family. Many of the cabins had been rebuilt and a few added and all now had electricity. They were rented out by the week and there were always new families with kids throughout the summer. Some of them returned the same time every year and I built some good friendships.

Dad would come during his vacation which was usually three weeks. He would fly into Escanaba where we would pick him up. We would hike the backcountry on two-track trails that went for miles circling around countless small lakes and ponds. We would head out after breakfast and come back to our cabin only for lunch and dinner. In the evening, someone would build a bonfire at the resort's beach and families would gather around and describe their adventures of the day or talk about whatever they felt like. These were the summers my dad taught me how to read a map and use a compass.

My grandpa had an old wooden speed boat (without the speed) that we would put in the lake every year. At one time it probably had a windshield but the boat's twenty-horsepower Evinrude motor couldn't go very fast so the wind wasn't a problem. I wasn't allowed to operate the motor until I was older but I could row it anytime I wanted. Because the boat was very heavy, I was in really good shape by the end of every summer.

⌐

IN THE SUMMER of 1962, after I completed ninth grade, we moved back to Michigan. My parents bought a home in Avon Township, just north of Troy. My grandparents had already moved to Troy and my mom wanted to be close and so our new home was just over a mile away.

Also not too far away was my new school. That September, I enrolled in Avondale High School where the first thing I learned was how to develop bad study habits. If they gave a grade in that I would have been valedictorian but instead I got mostly B's and C's, although I did enjoy my high school days. I was accepted at Oakland University despite my C-plus average because I achieved high scores on the entrance exam.

When I got to college, there was a price to be paid for those bad study habits. Studying was challenging for me at Oakland University, but again I enjoyed being a student even though my outside interests didn't leave much time for study. Among other things, I swam on the varsity swim team, worked several part-time jobs on campus, and played guitar for the evening folk masses at St John's Chapel across University Boulevard from the Oakland University campus. One good decision I made was to take Charter College which sponsored the first study abroad program at Oakland University.

Before I arrived for my first classes at Oakland, I had volunteered for a new program called Charter College. Colleges within universities had become the new rage. Usually they recruited exceptional students but the professors at Oakland wanted to experiment with a cross section of students with a variety of academic abilities which is how I was accepted.

At the initial introduction, the professors who were leading this program gave us the following criteria for courses. We would have the freedom to pick any area of study as long as it fit University requirements and a professor could be found to teach it. All the courses would be non-graded, strictly pass or fail. Within a few minutes of this presentation a student stood up and asked if we could do a study-abroad semester. The professors seemed perplexed but answered yes, but provided that there would be a planning committee as well as professors willing to teach the courses. The Charter College professors thought the study-abroad idea would die in committee. That did not happen.

Sixteen months later, in January 1967, sixty of us left for Europe on Icelandic Airlines. I was embarking on an experience that changed my life.

We broke into three groups that would rotate between Paris, Mainz (Germany) and Madrid. We took a week traveling in between. There were three professors along with their families, each stationed in one of the three cities. Dr. Lessing and his family were in Paris, Dr. Cherno was in Mainz and Dr. Burdick and his wife were in Madrid.

I earned the money for the trip the summer of 1966 working the afternoon shift at Pontiac Motors. My job was putting the pistons into the engine block on the line. We worked 60-hour weeks and with overtime, the money added up quickly. I worked the very hot afternoon shift and came home soaked in oil. After several weeks my skin developed a rash. After two months I had saved almost enough money for my trip, so I was able to quit Pontiac Motors to take a job as camp counselor for the Detroit YMCA Camp Ohiyesa, on the shores of Fish Lake in Holly, a job I loved.

I traveled to Europe on a very strict budget. The whole trip cost me just over five thousand dollars. This included air fare, all the transfers between cities, breakfasts and dinners, lodging for three-and-one-half months and twelve credit hours at Oakland. Throughout this time, I did a lot of walking and occasionally hitchhiking and had experiences worthy of a book all by themselves. There was a significant downside—by this time my course work at Oakland was on life support and I was not looking forward to the next semester.

I had realized during the semester in Europe that being away from home had made some real differences, not the least of which was in my academic abilities. There would be more than the usual consequences, because this was the Vietnam War era and that meant quitting school would in turn mean being drafted. By the end of the fall semester of 1967 I knew I had to do something so in January 1968 I made a major decision to join the Coast Guard. But the waiting list then for the Coast Guard was nine months, so I stayed at Oakland for the winter semester even though studying was next to impossible for me. No surprise that I did not do well and at the end of the semester I was academically dismissed for a year.

Just after my twenty-first birthday, in early October 1968, I finally got my orders for the Guard. Soon thereafter came my draft orders but I had already started basic training in Cape May, New Jersey. I had really dodged a bullet.

I READ WITH interest the enticing brochure the Coast Guard recruiting officer had given me about the basic training facility at Cape May, New Jersey. It featured recreational facilities with television sets and I looked forward to being in training during the day, after which I would amble over to a lounge area in the evening to watch TV. By a nice coincidence the Detroit Tigers were playing in the 1968 World Series and I really did not want to miss that. Reality intervened. It would be nine weeks before I even saw a TV again. I may have averaged about three-and-a-half hours of sleep a night. However, I did learn two lessons. First, I could actually nap standing up. Second, I could tolerate considerable abuse. One example: I looked forward to my visits to the dentist where I could nap in the dental chair for twenty minutes before the dentist came in to work on my teeth.

Several weeks into basic training we took the Naval Battery Exams to identify aptitudes and determine the schools for which we would qualify. Even though I kept dozing off during the exams, I scored so well I was given my choice of schools and even qualified for Aviation Cadet School. That would have meant a seven-year commitment and even so I would have chosen that option. However, there were were no openings at the time so instead I chose the nine-month Naval Sonar School in Key West, Florida.

I finished basic training just before the holidays, and was given liberty until the beginning of January. I flew down to Miami where I met up with another Coast Guard Seaman, Guy Johnston, also on his way to Sonar School. We quickly became very close friends and together took a puddle jumper to Key West, arriving as the evening sun lit a warm glow on the horizon and a light breeze wafted through the palm trees. I understood at once why Ernest Hemingway spent so much time here. For the first time, life in the military was delightful.

The Naval Sonar School was good duty, especially the electronics classes. I attended classes weekdays from 8 a.m. to 4 p.m., stood watch several times a week, and the rest of the time was mostly my own.

Key West is a coral island and there is a coral reef along the Atlantic Side of the Keys. At Key West the reef is five to seven miles off shore. Several of my friends and I spent a number of weekends free diving the reefs. After a while I was able to hold my breath for over two minutes and could dive forty-five feet and work the floor for about forty-five seconds.

There were two German Navy students in my class and we became good friends. Guy and the Germans and I were all over twenty-one and spent several evenings a week at the Enlisted Men's Club drinking beer. The German Navy at that time had a daily ration (liquor) for their enlisted members. Because they were not assigned to a German facility, our German buddies would get a Care package once a month with their whole monthly allotment of liquor and were the only students allowed to keep booze in their rooms. Guy and I were invited several times to visit and share their Courvoisier Brandy.

There are times when an event happens that has so much impact that we will remember forever that very moment and where we were. One Sunday evening, July 20, 1969, I was in the EM Club sitting by myself as I ate a hamburger and fries with a beer. I looked up to see on the television screen as Neil Armstrong stepped off the Eagle onto the Moon. To this day I compare all hamburgers to that hamburger at the EM Club in Key West—none has ever tasted as good.

A month later I graduated from Sonar School at the top of my class and was given my choice of duty stations. My close friend Guy was from Carlsbad, California and he wanted to go back home. Of the four openings in Long Beach, I chose Long Beach and offered to trade with Guy, if he did not get Long Beach. We both ended up in Long Beach on the 256-foot Weather Cutter *Minnetonka*. The *Minnetonka* had just came back from Vietnam and the other ship that we could have been assigned was about ready to go to Vietnam. Until that moment, I was unaware the Coast Guard had troops in Vietnam.

Ironically, two weeks before we boarded the *Minnetonka* the sonar equipment had been removed because it was locat-

ed far below decks in the belly of the ship where sonar equipment would need air conditioning to stay functional. Because
the over-heating sonar was constantly breaking down, instead of maintaining equipment and standing sonar watches,
I spent my time while we were at sea doing two daily four-
hour radar watches, acting as Comtac Publication Librarian,
and performing oceanographic casting to collect water sam-
ples from various ocean depths.

While I was on board the *Minnetonka*, we did two Ocean
Station operations between San Francisco and Hawaii and
two Ocean Station operations between Midway and Japan.
We would be on Ocean Station for three weeks before being
relieved by another ship. When we did the Ocean Stations between Midway and Japan, we sailed to Japan to refuel and get
provisions for our second Ocean Station.

I was kept very busy aboard the ship and was not happy
when in addition to everything else, our Chief Petty Officer
made me swab decks. But I was pleasantly surprised when
this chore worked to my advantage. We had pulled into Yoko-
suka, Japan for resupplying before going back to Ocean Station Victor. Perhaps our Duty Officer in charge of the radar
group felt sorry for me because I was granted ten days liberty
which did not count against my leave time. I used it to travel
in Japan, visiting Nikko, a National Park North of Tokyo and
also spent time in Tokyo where I met a business student from
the University of Tokyo. I spent several days with him and his
friends who introduced me to sashimi (thinly sliced raw fish),
cold seaweed soup and excellent sake at a sushi house.

I was on board *Minnetonka* for just over a year before I
was transferred to shore duty stationed at Captain of the Port
Office in Long Beach. There I was involved with oil pollution
investigation and also dispatching. There were no long-term
sleeping accommodations available so I was given a stipend

to live off base. Eventually I found an apartment I really liked, two blocks from the ocean just south of the commercial area of Long Beach. The building was an old California court with an open yard enclosed by apartments. I had a living room, one bedroom and a closet-sized kitchen.

Guy had also been transferred to shore duty at the Coast Guard Recruiting Office in Long Beach. We would get together once in a while at a local bar called Hogan's East where Guy introduced me to Vern and Carol who worked at the local Sears Store. One night they invited me to a "Sears Party" on the weekend at Vern's little apartment over a detached garage with wooden stairs and railing going up the side. When I arrived, I was astonished to see people hanging over the rickety stairs and then to see that inside it was wall-to-wall people dancing. I have never really enjoyed crowds and was overwhelmed. But right away Carol greeted me and introduced me to several people, including a tall, attractive girl.

As I sat at a stool in the living room watching everyone dancing, I finally got up the courage to ask one girl to dance, but she did not seem very interested in me. However, after a while that tall young lady that Carol had first introduced me to came over and started talking with me. We ended up talking through the rest of the evening and into the early morning. She was working part time at Sears and going to Long Beach State College while working on her masters in fabric design. She also had her teaching certificate and was substitute teaching. Her name was Joan Malfitano. What began in that crowded apartment at a party was chapter one in what could be a book all of its own, for four months later we got married. Joan has said she thought it was her cooking that attracted me to her. Yes, her cooking is really amazing, but it was her intelligence and her sense of adventure that I really admired and still do to this day.

I had just a year left in the Coast Guard after we were married. We moved back to Michigan in August of 1972 so I could finish my degree in sociology at Oakland University. The GI Bill helped pay for school and I worked full time at a plastics factory in the summer. Joan was working as a substitute in the Troy school district and hoping for a full-time position as an art teacher.

Obviously much had changed as I matured during my Coast Guard years, because I did much better in school and finally graduated in May of 1974. My first job was with the Michigan Department of Mental Health at Clinton Valley Center, working with emotionally disturbed teens. Later I would transfer to Oakdale Center for Developmental Disabilities working with Senior Adults as a program monitor.

Joan did not get the Art Teaching position but six weeks later with an eight-hundred-dollar investment we opened a jewelry store in a small room on a side street in Clarkston, Michigan. We bought casting equipment and other jewelry supplies and Joan made sterling silver rings and took handmade gift items on consignment. Within a month Joan was also fabricating silver and brass earrings and pendants and a year later we were moving into a space on Main Street. Seven years after opening, I came into the business full time.

~

IN 1995 WE opened a B&B in Clarkston—we named it Millpond Inn. Since day one, this has been an incredibly rewarding experience as we have opened our door to people from all over the world, bringing to our town and our home their diverse backgrounds, occupations, and perspectives on life. Stimulating discussions at breakfast touch on health, politics, religion, economics, travel, occupational experiences and much, much more because we have hosted authors, actors, entertainers,

treasure hunters, politicians, lawyers, professors, research-
ers, executives, medical professionals, race care drivers, professional athletes and—not least— very interesting ordinary
people that often are so much more than ordinary.

However, this steady infusion of fresh insight as I approach age sixty-nine inevitably poses a question for me, a
question I have yet to answer: with so many fascinating options open to me, what should I choose for my next career?

~11~

LEARNING TO TEACH...
TEACHING TO LEARN
by Mel Vaara

*"I've been blessed, with family, education, career,
sports, spiritual growth, and amazing people
I've encountered along the way."*

IT TOOK A hard-earned five dollars to bring me into the world. It was August 1933, the depth of The Great Depression. There was no hospital and even if there had been there was very little money. So, at a cost of that precious five dollars, a doctor came to my grandparents' farm house in Bessemer Township, between Wakefield and Ironwood in the Upper Peninsula. Years earlier, it had been to that rural area of Michigan, just east of the Wisconsin state border, that my maternal grandparents, Eliina Sophia and Victor Stengard, had immigrated from Finland.

Grandfather worked in the iron ore mines while Grandmother kept the home fires burning in the fullest sense of that expression, raising a family of six daughters and two sons, along with gardening and caring for the animals.

My father, John Hilding, arrived from Sweden at age seventeen, with his two brothers, Frank and Oscar. In the chaos and confusion of hordes of immigrants arriving, people often ended up with new last names. Frank kept his original name, Turovaara, while my Dad eliminated the "Turo." Uncle Oscar, for some unknown reason, changed his name to Berg.

After I was born, we moved to Puritan, a small mining community where the company owned all the homes. But soon there was a danger of cave-ins, so everybody had to find other places to live. My parents were lucky enough to buy a home in what was called The Resettlement. It was one of the Works Project Administration (WPA) projects that President Franklin Delano Roosevelt created to put people back to work during the Depression years before World War II.

The Resettlement had one hundred and thirty-six homes, black-top streets, sewers, water, softball and baseball fields, tennis courts, a raft pond, and ski-jumping facility. It also had a community building, post office, and grocery store. We had all those amenities at a cost of seventeen dollars a month. All of those homes are still standing and in good shape, a testament to one of the many great accomplishments of the FDR Administration.

Childhood was filled with good times with my three brothers, Robert, Carl, and John David (who all followed me in careers in education) and with many friends from the neighborhood and our church, Saint Paul's Evangelical Lutheran in Ironwood. Welch Creek, running upstream from the raft pond, was filled with brook trout, so we would take potatoes and a salt shaker and walk to the creek. There, with our bare hands, we pulled out trout, then cleaned and gutted them. We built a fire from found wood and over that crackling campfire we cooked the best-tasting trout ever.

In the winter we went skiing, cutting old tire inner tubes to make ski bindings that broke often, but that was okay because we had already stashed spare bindings around our arms. We also spent countless hours playing unsupervised basketball in the Community Building Gymnasium with few big arguments, no real fights, and no lasting hard feelings.

Church was a central feature of life in Puritan. I taught Sunday School and assumed leadership in Luther League to junior and senior high school youth. Most everyone helped out with that trademark upstate Michigan community activity—pasty sales. At Christmas time, each child received a bag of candy. My brothers and I helped the custodian take down the Christmas tree and for that we each got another bag of candy.

We were poor, but as that condition was so common then, we didn't think of ourselves as poor because everyone else was poor, too. I attended township schools through ninth grade, then transferred to Luther L. Wright High School in Ironwood, graduating in 1951. That school had been built as another WPA project and is as elegant today as when it was built.

At the time, I was unaware I was experiencing discrimination for the first time. The "city kids" had more money, were better dressed, had cars, and always appeared to have the better teachers and the advanced classes. I felt a bit the outsider, but even so, high school was a happy learning experience, in great part because I had some outstanding coaches. I ran track and cross county, and became manager of the varsity basketball team.

Our coach, S.F. Goedde, was tall and imposing and went by the nickname, "Stretch." He was fair but very firm. Once we forgot to bring the uniforms to Hurley, Wisconsin for the big Hurley-Ironwood game. Coach Goedde yelled, "I don't know how you're going to do it, but those uniforms better be here by game time." We pleaded with the bus driver to rush us back to Ironwood. Somehow we got there, picked up the uniforms, and made it back for the start of the game—an indelible lesson learned.

I must have inherited my work ethic from my parents. I began babysitting jobs at age eleven for neighbors and relatives. I got my first summer job at age fourteen at a small gas station near my home, earning one dollar a day. The next summer, my salary was increased to thirty-five dollars a week.

My senior year, in 1950, I joined the National Guard, and that proved to be another positive influence on my educational journey. After graduation from high school, I attended Gogebic Junior College which happened to be housed on the third floor of the high school building. Fewer than a hundred students were enrolled and I was able to attend only because I had received an athletic scholarship of fifty dollars a semester. That scholarship money was important because my new job at OK Auto Parts paid only one dollar an hour.

Whatever situation I found myself in, I began to realize that I was successful in roles where I took the lead. I was elected chairman of the Snow Bowl Carnival, not only a fun occasion for the school and community, but also a huge responsibility to manage.

After completing junior college, I transferred to Northern Michigan University in Marquette to finish up my junior and senior years. My parents drove me to Marquette and as they left, my Mom reached through the car window and handed me a five-dollar bill. I stared at it, knowing that it probably left her with nothing for coffee and donuts for the week.

I continued working at OK Auto Parts and that meant hitchhiking home on Fridays to work all day on Saturdays. After making my eight bucks, I would hitchhike back on Sunday. Doing the math, I could see that out of the eight dollars income, five went to rent, leaving three dollars for food for the week. By Thursday, I was playing cards to earn something to buy a meal on Friday, usual a pasty pie and chocolate milk.

⟿

My FIRST DAY at NMU, I walked into a huge arena. It was jammed with athletes, students, and teachers having a great old time and here was little ol' Mel with a dime in his pocket, enough for a Coke. As I stood there feeling sorry for myself, up came a fellow to welcome me. His name was Tom Peters, inviting me to sit with him and his friends. It was one of life's sweet moments—and I resolved then and there that I would do the same for others. No way of knowing then, but Tom Peters would one day become Vice President of NMU.

For preparing students for a wide variety of careers, NMU has done an excellent job. My two years flew by. I was on the track team, running the half-mile, mile and two-mile races in one day. My two-mile time may still stand. I joined a fraternity, the N Club, and Future Teachers of Michigan. The enduring legacy is the excellent instructors and coaches I was fortunate to have.

As graduation approached and job interviewing began, I set a goal of teaching in the Upper Peninsula. I was offered a contract from Escanaba for twenty-eight hundred dollars a year and that sounded just fine to me. But then Dr. Lesley F. Greene of Clarkston Community Schools interviewed me and offered thirty-two hundred. I was content with the Escanaba offer and told Dr. Greene I wasn't interested. A week later, I received a registered letter from him raising the offer another three hundred dollars, with a cover letter saying simply, "Sign here and send back."

Feeling somehow that the Lord convinced me to move to Clarkston, that is what I did. I knew nothing about the school system or the area; there was no Highway I-75 or a Big Mac Bridge to ease the way; and affordable housing was a problem for educators, but it was one of the best decisions I ever made.

Fortunately, Dr. Greene was resourceful at getting teachers situated. He introduced me to a widow, Mrs. Seeterlin, whose husband had owned a local car dealership, and she rented me a room for ten dollars a week, including breakfast and laundry.

It didn't take me long to learn the history of Clarkston, a "Henry Ford town," to appreciate the diversity and beauty of the area. I quickly recognized that the community was vibrant economically and that the families of my students were strong and solid people.

In 1955, the administration office was housed in Clarkston Elementary School, with Andersonville being the only other elementary school—Pine Knob was under construction. The Junior and Senior High School classes were together in the building that has since been beautifully renovated as Renaissance High School.

I was the first male elementary teacher in Clarkston. I had thirty-five kids in my sixth-grade classroom and our only extra was a music teacher. There was no cafeteria so we ate lunch in our classroom. We spent a lot of time outside, playing soccer and softball. Some of those students of more than fifty years ago still send me cards and letters.

As exciting as it was to be in this new role and learning about Clarkston and the surrounding area, the best was yet to come.

One Sunday morning, I arrived home from church driving my new 1956 red-and-white Chevrolet, just as Josephine (nick-named Jo) Nickora was coming home from church. Jo lived two doors down from me where she rented a room at the beautiful home of a widow, Mrs. Rowena O'Dell. I said, "How about taking a ride in my new car to meet some of my friends at Michigan State?" Six months later, we were engaged.

⌒

IN JUNE 1957, I married the person who has been the single greatest influence in my life.

Jo continued to teach and for two years, I taught elementary school and then was offered a job teaching Junior High math and physical education and coaching Junior Varsity basketball and Varsity track, as well as High School cross-country. Success came quickly: my basketball team went undefeated and I appeared likely to fill the opening job as Varsity coach. I was disappointed when that didn't happen for what appeared to be political reasons but Dr. Greene assured me that I would be better off financially to pursue an administrative career track instead of being a coach. Soon he installed me as Assistant Principal at Clarkston Junior High.

After several enjoyable years in that role, I was surprised when Dr. Greene called me to his office to share unusual and surprising information. Unexpectedly, the Junior High principal had to step down due to personal problems and, effective at once, I was named to succeed him. My training for that role consisted of being told, "Just do what you are supposed to do."

For two years, that is just what I did. Then, once again I was called in and told more unexpected news and given a new assignment. I was to be Principal of a new Junior High to be built on Sashabaw Road and would work with the architect, hire the teachers, and set up the curriculum. And, oh yes, have it all ready by the summer of 1969. We did it and in 2006, the Board of Education honored me by naming the gymnasium the Mel Vaara Gymnasium, with nearly all of the original Sashabaw Junior High staff attending the ceremonies.

After two years as Sashabaw Junior High Principal, I took the added responsibility for both junior highs. The next year saw a promotion to Assistant Superintendent with chief responsibilities as Curriculum Director. When I asked what a Curriculum Director does, Dr. Greene replied, "I don't know; that's why I hired you." But I quickly learned it was indeed a big job, with responsibility for curriculum, administrators, teachers, all school personnel, child accounting, and vocational education. I loved it, in part because the challenges were as great as the needs and I got outstanding support from all the administrators.

During that time, I also served as President of the Oakland County Curriculum Council. I began to get involved in other community ventures and was elected Trustee of Independence Township for eight years. After I retired, I ran for Supervisor and lost in a very close election by a hundred and fifty votes.

~

In 1992, after Clarkston Schools hired a new Superintendent, I decided to retire, convinced I wouldn't be able to work effectively with him. New opportunities beckoned, and soon I was in exciting roles at Huron Valley Schools, then Holly School District. Oakland Schools called me to be Principal of their Tech Center. And I was called back to work for Sashabaw Junior High for several months. In all these roles, I enjoyed working with several different superintendents. It was good to make an impact, to feel appreciated, and, occasionally to be well compensated for my efforts.

My last job was a departure from what I had long done. I was Principal of a private Lutheran Elementary School, Saint Stephens in Waterford. In my two years there, I brought a public school influence into their school system. The pastor was dismayed about that, and he judged my curriculum to be much too liberal, which it unapologetically was. Still, I left a mark there and made many new friends.

Jo and I have continued to be involved in community service whenever we feel we can make a contribution, where we can make a difference. We have been fortunate because we have gained so very much by being allowed to turn our talents and our hands to helping others. I belong to SCAMP, the summer school for special needs youngsters and served as its president for two years. For twenty-five years I was a member of Optimists Club. A real privilege was being chosen as committee chair when we built the last addition onto Calvary Evangelical Lutheran Church. For more than two decades, I enjoyed serving as a high school basketball referee, handling some big-time games with boys who became outstanding college players, including Clarkston's own Dan Fife.

After all North Michigan University has done for me with a solid education, I was honored to be appointed by the NMU President to serve on the Board of Directors for Alumni Relations for seven years. Later I was selected to receive the outstanding alumnus award, and Jo and I were called on to help select a new President for NMU.

~~

IN 1973, WHEN the Pine Knob resort complex was seeking approvals, I had become Chairman of the Planning Commission and the Board of Appeals. The site was an historic one. In the 1920s, a very private man, Colonel Sydney Waldon, built a mansion on Pine Knob. That peak, at 1,201 feet was considered, at the time, to be the highest point in southeast Michigan. He had intended the place as his bachelor retreat, but he soon remarried and kept the mansion extremely private for his family's exclusive use. After he died, his widow sold the property to Ford Hospital, which coveted the seclusion of the place as a last resting place for terminally ill patients. It eventually became the Pine Knob Nursing Home.

To say that the proposed development of this special property was controversial would be to greatly understate it. We had nightly meetings, meetings that lasted late into the evening. The owner who was proposing this elaborate project and significant investment was a brilliant man named Joe Locricchio who cut quite the elegant figure, featuring a different designer suit or flashy leather jacket at every meeting. Locricchio had two lofty goals. One was for Pine Knob to become a magnificent, world-class golf course where legends like Jack Nicklaus and Arnold Palmer would tread the fairways. While the three nine-hole courses in the complex eventually matured into decent tests, the layout never achieved that lofty stature. The second goal was to have a high-class hotel and a ski jump.

After prolonged haggling and tense moments, the decision came down to me. I had intense pressure from the public, most of whom wanted neither the hotel nor the ski jump. I voted against it and have wondered countless times whether that was, after all, the best decision, even though a majority may have wanted it not to be built. It could have been a monumental engineering feat. Perhaps it could have become the centerpiece of Independence Township. Then again, it may well have never come to fruition anyhow, because Locricchio ran out of money and then died at a young age. Ultimately, the property was sold and it was left to others to develop.

One of my duties as chairman was to attend ceremonies, such as grand openings and major milestone events. So, Jo and I were in front-row seats at the premiere event at Pine Knob Music Theater, a concert featuring The Carpenters. Our daughter Anne Marie was then a sophomore at Clarkston High School and a drummer in the band. When Karen Carpenter threw her drum sticks out into the audience, Anne Marie caught one.

Things were picking up for Anne Marie in other ways, too. Specifically—trash, and there was a lot of it to pick up at Pine Knob where she had landed her first job. In her junior year, she became chairwoman of all the committees for trash removal and eventually worked her way up to become theater manager. Through that job, Anne Marie brought us into contact with many performing artists. I was pressed into duty as a notary public when Willie Nelson needed something notarized. Jo and I entered Willie's bus where a couple dozen people seemed all to be smoking something that went unnamed but certainly was providing happy moods. Meandering to the back of the bus, we found Willie who thanked us for coming and handed me the papers for stamping with my notary seal. As we began to leave, he handed me several one hundred dollar bills. "Thanks, but there is no charge for this," I said, and handed him back the money. He was stunned but quickly said he would make sure we had great seats and a good time.

During the concert, Willie was so relaxed, so cool. When a spaced-out fan clambered up onto the stage and made a grand fool of himself, Willie just let him ramble on until he was ushered gently back to his seat.

A much different atmosphere surrounded the Frank Sinatra concert, beginning with his arrival in a helicopter very shortly before he was scheduled to be on stage. Out he came, pale blue leisure suit, puka-shell necklace dangling from his neck. Like every Sinatra performance, an indelible memory.

Another phone call brought an unusual request. It was singer Anne Murray in need of blankets for her children so they could sleep backstage. Next was Olivia Newton-John who was staying in a Pine Knob condo that had no draperies. She needed sheets to use as temporary drapes so she could sleep in late.

The list went on—experiences with Joan Rivers, Barry

Manilow and so many others. In addition to Anne Marie, our other three daughters—Liisa, Ingrid, and Tasha—all had jobs at Pine Knob while in high school. All have gone on to careers in helping professions.

⁓

RUMMAGING THROUGH THE eight decades of my life has proved to be both a challenge and a treasure hunt. So many jobs, so many memories to get into focus and to get into the right sequence. A lot of material, a lot of events, a lot of living to account for, and yet several things stand starkly out. Jo, of course, sweetheart, companion, counselor, conscience—so much a part of me that I scarcely know where Mel ends and Jo begins. That bond has produced four daughters that would make any parent proud and humble at the same time. All four educated at Michigan State. All four chose careers in helping professions; one as CEO of Clinton River Watershed; one as a social worker; one an occupational therapist; one a speech pathologist.

The beat goes on, with six lively grandchildren with sports and school functions that keep their grandparents young at heart, if not always in body. The cliches about grandchildren are cliches simply because they are all too true: they grow up so fast that every moment with them must be savored, must be treasured because too soon childhood, then adolescence, will be memories only, as are mine of a farm house in Bessemer Township, of cooking brook trout by a campfire.

Each life story is, after all, a unique tapestry of experiences. For me, I've been blessed, with family, education, career, sports, spiritual growth, and amazing people I've encountered along the way. The stories of some of those people are told, in great part for the first time, in the chapters of this book. These are men and women I have come to know in these later years. How such disparate folks came to know one another is recounted in the last pages of this book. These late-blooming friendships are proof of the strange and wonderful role that chance plays in our lives. Every one of these people is a forward-thinking person who has a burning desire to leave this planet a decent place for our grandchildren and for all who come after us.

Which brings us to why we wrote this book. The reasons are elaborated on in the first pages of this volume. As for me, I will just say simply that we feel that each of us lived our lives as best we could, that we tried to do things that contributed to our communities, that made a positive and perhaps a lasting difference. If I'm right about that, then these were stories worth telling. But I've been an educator long enough to know that it's best to let others make such judgments for themselves.

HOLDING COURT AT THE ROUND TABLE
&
BREWING A BOOK AT BRIONI CAFE

Several of the geezers who gather faithfully every Monday morning at the round table at Brioni Cafe & Deli are very serious gardeners. The rest of us admire and respect them not only because they grow great vegetables and give healthy produce to the needy, but also because they garden organically. Organic is good and locally grown organic is the best of all.

The group itself—and, eventually, this book—also grew organically. How the core group came into existence was not in the least planned, and somehow it seems almost ordained that, one by one, we would come together.

On July 2, 2012, at 9 a.m., Dale Bond (who keeps careful notes on his calendars about such things) went to Brioni's to sit with Bob McGowan, have a cup of coffee, and talk about whatever problems in the county, the state, and the world most needed their attention. They sat at the same round table that eventually came to be known by other Brioni's regulars as the table "where those geezers with all the progressive ideas hold forth every Monday morning."

As they wrapped up their wide-ranging conversation, finished their coffee, and got up from the table, Dale said, "We should do this more often." To which Bob replied, "Good idea."

Without them knowing it, at that moment the cornerstone was laid in the foundation upon which would be built something more substantial, extending onward and upward to more than two hundred Monday mornings, and counting.

A couple weeks later, Bob brought along his fellow organic gardeners, Wally Niezguski and Chris Reading. They had occasionally met for coffee in other spots in the area but until they landed in Brioni's, nothing felt quite so right. Soon thereafter, Mel Vaara and Jerry McNally happened by, listened in a bit, then sat down and quickly joined in.

To that original core, Buck Kopietz, Dennis Ritter, Jim Reed, and Carole Cotter Bodner brought fresh backgrounds and experiences along with the same progressive points of view and value systems.

Everyone liked to bring something fresh and stimulating every Monday morning, but also came prepared to listen, to learn something new, or to hear a different slant on what was going on in Michigan and in the country.

Bill Haney, last to sit in, likewise was bent the same way politically but also brought long experience as a writer and book publisher. In early 2015, Bill mentioned to his son Mark he was enjoying the round table group at Brioni's and told him a bit about the people. Mark said it sounded to him as if they had stories to tell about how it was growing up in those turbulent days of their younger years. The question naturally arose: Would they enjoy getting those stories recorded for posterity, perhaps with a little about what came afterwards for them? If they answer was yes, why not do a book?

Why not, indeed.

That is how the group came together and how this book came to be. This book has told something of how each of these authors started out in life, about what was going on in the communities in which they lived. It gives an unretouched picture of life under the storm clouds over the greater world as they progressed from childhood, through teenage years, and into adulthood. These pages offer some insight and context about what occupied them before traveling long and winding roads to one day find themselves sharing coffee and muffins at Brioni Cafe & Deli in Clarkston every Monday morning.

Fittingly, this book is much like the group itself—it was grown organically and locally.

Acknowledgments & Appreciations

THE AUTHORS EXPRESS their gratitude for helping hands, support, and encouragement of those named below. We thank the many others who lent a hand, offered encouragement, or just remained patient and understanding throughout.

First, of course, we must mention the fine people of Brioni Cafe & Deli, presided over by Larry and Louise Stakle, and son Robert. We thank and applaud their cordial, capable staff, including Meghan Graney who doubled as photographer to capture the image of the group reproduced herein. Without their warm hospitality and their indulgence of our domination of the Round Table every Monday morning—not to mention their super coffee and baked goods—this book simply would never have come into existence.

A frequent topic of discussion every week is the state of our state of Michigan and that leads, of course, to reflecting on the visionary leadership of former Governor Jennifer Granholm during eight of the most challenging and politically divisive years this state has seen. So, we are grateful, yet again, to former Governor Granholm for the generous sentiments in her Foreword.

Writing the words for a book is one thing. Making it a physical reality is another. As she has done so deftly for many authors, Jacinta Calcut of Image Graphics & Design created the jacket design and montage of images printed on the end leaves, and produced text composition, supported and counseled by Ken Calcut's business and technical expertise.

Carole Cotter Bodner, author of her own chapter, has said she has enjoyed the opportunity to be a part of this venture, but cannot possibly be as grateful as her fellow authors are for her sharp proofreading eye that caught many gremlins before they made it to the printed page.

Loraine Campbell, Executive Director of Troy Historical

Village, and Elizabeth Thornburg of the THV staff, provided vintage images in Oakland County from the 1930-50s which are used in the end leaves of this volume, along with materials provided by the authors themselves.

Because this book is a memoir, it necessarily draws off the memories of its authors, reaching back many decades. We have endeavored to be accurate and to verify what we have written wherever possible. To do that, we have checked the documented historical record, where it exists, and also have turned to the recollections of others as fact-checkers. Dick Halsey, long-time resident of Oakland County, is typical of those who corrected our memories, along with many other people too numerous to mention, but to whom we are indebted.

While many people had a hand in the book itself, others contributed to the project in different and important ways. Kari Roehl and Shelly Glass, out of an excess of kindness to others, provided invaluable help at the book launch event.

As for the authors themselves, they know full well they did not make this journey alone.

Mel Vaara readily gives his heartfelt thanks and appreciation to his wife, Jo Nickora-Vaara, daughters Anne Marie, Liisa Jo, Ingrid Helen, Tasha Linnea, their loving partners Jeff, Carl, Chris, Lisa and six beautiful grandchildren, Nickora, Mackay, Claudia, Eric, Nolan, and Fiona. They have brought so much laughter and joy and now, in my later years, helpfulness, concern and compassion. Mine really has been "A Wonderful Life."

Bob McGowan gladly confirms that all he has come to be has been shaped by his wonderful wife, Barbara, and the support of son Jason and daughter Lucy, son-in-law Piero and, most lately, his grandchildren, Madeline, Olivia and Mia.

However, Bob McGowan is a not only a giver of thanks but also a recipient. The family of Chris Reading thanks Bob for his efforts on the chapter about Chris. Chris's wife Gail, his sons, John, Grant, David, and Paul, and their families are grateful for Bob's kind and thoughtful words, his dear friendship to Chris, and for keeping Chris's memory alive.

Jerry McNally appreciates greatly the help he received from wife Carol in reading and typing his chapter, not to mention everything else she has done, which would take a long list.

Buck Kopietz's life changed the moment he met Joan Malfitano who became his wife, partner, personal chef, and companion in adventure, and object of his admiration and appreciation forever.

Dale Bond was aided in getting his story together by his wife, Nancy Bond, and grandson Nicholas Scott.

Dennis Ritter is grateful to his wife Sandy for her understanding and help as he worked on his chapter and for making him proud of her many contributions to communities she has so ably served.

Wally Niezguski is keenly aware he would not have been able to produce his chapter, nor the most fruitful years of his life, without Dollie at his side every step of the way, often sacrificing time from her own careers to help him in his.

Jim Reed's story would have been much different without the decades of support from his wife, Barbara, and their children who made it a great life with wonderful memories.

Bill Haney's life continues to be a work in process at the hands of wife Marcy (she who must be obeyed); children Mark, Jennifer, Rebecca, and Jessica; and grandchildren Meghan, Gillian, Robin, Jerome, Zacharie, Amelie, Elliott and Annika, several of whom lent a hand during this project, and son Patrick, whose spirit infuses and inspires us all.

Inevitably, we will have unintentionally failed to acknowledge or thank someone who has helped along the way, in the making of this book, or in the making of a full and rich life. As they read the pages of this book, we hope they will smile and see where they have nonetheless left their own fingerprints on these pages and in our lives.

Monday Morning Authors
of
One Cup at a Time

Bill Haney

Wally Niezguski

Dale Bond

Jerry McNally

Jim Reed

Gail Reading

Dennis Ritter

Bob McGowan

Carole Cotter Bodner

Buck Kopietz

Mel Vaara

PHOTOGRAPH BY MEGAN GRANEY

Dennis Ritter, the eighth child in family of 12 kids, was raised in Pontiac, served in the U.S. Army in Ethiopia and Vietnam, and survived the TET Offensive. An OCC and University of Michigan graduate, he became a small business owner and was deeply involved in Democratic politics, serving as a delegate to the 1984 Democratic National Convention. A collector of political campaign memorabilia, he served over thirty years as an elected and appointed public official.

Bob McGowan grew up in Rochester, Michigan, did a B.A. and M.A. at Oakland University, and taught English, French and drama for nine years. He was an advertising writer for three-plus decades, has written a couple of books and published several others, and founded a charitable garden he has executive directed for twenty-five years.

Dale Bond, born and grew up in Detroit, USAF veteran, Independence Township resident since 1963, saw his six children graduate from Clarkston school. After decades as an inventor and manufacturing plant owner, now is an avid area historian, barn preservationist, and genealogist.

Mel Vaara, born and raised in Ironwood, Michigan, graduated from Gogebic Junior College, received a B.S. degree from Northern Michigan University, and an M.A. from Michigan State University. He spent his entire career— almost 40 years—with Clarkston Community Schools.

Jerry McNally's life has been a pilgrimage, with ports of call from Nebraska to Greenland. He presided for thirty-four years as a District Court judge. During his working years, he investigated the material world, while in his retirement he is investigating the immaterial world.

Bill Haney, ever in search of the meaning of life after Big Beaver days, took a B.A. from the University of Michigan, worked on lunar exploration projects, was on the UM staff for ten years, and was a corporate officer for communications and marketing companies. He wrote several books and published many other authors in companies he established.

Carole Cotter Bodner, born in Detroit, grew up in Troy, and taught six years, but yearned to travel and to live in a warmer climate. Migrating into the computer world, she lived in California and Virginia. Back again in Michigan, she grows vegetables in a community garden for the Gleaners food bank.

Jim Reed, a lifetime Michigander, was born in Flint, became a GM family person, married a Flint girl, is a serious birder and duplicate bridge player, and still loves Michigan outdoors.

Wally Niezguski, careened around North America in a dizzying array of occupations, yet returned again and again to Michigan to finally settle on a farm on Sashabaw Road where he produces organic vegetables and free range eggs, a mere half hour from his Ferndale birthplace.

Buck Kopietz was born in the U.P. of Michigan and grew up in Detroit, Albuquerque, and Avon Township. He graduated from Oakland University and owned two businesses in Clarkston with his wife, Joan. He is currently promoting a paradigm shift in healthcare concentrating on prevention.

Gail Reading, wife, soulmate, and devoted partner of Chris Reading who was a founder of the Original Six who formed the core of what grew into the Brioni bunch.

The authors are honored to be able to donate to Reading Works a share of proceeds for every copy sold of this book to help in their crucial efforts to raise adult literacy in Michigan.

ONE IN THREE adults in Michigan reads at or below a fifth-grade level—twice the national average. These adults qualify for only 10 percent of new jobs. Children of parents who can't read are 87 percent more likely to be living in poverty.

Reading Works is dedicated to raising the level of adult literacy in metro Detroit and promoting the idea that Reading Works—in the family and in the workplace. We believe adult literacy is the gateway issue because it can improve every facet of our community's social and economic well-being.

Reading Works has formed a collective of local literacy providers (Impact Partners) with proven expertise and success to advance adult literacy across the region in ways each could not do alone. The pillars of the Reading Works strategy are: Awareness to demonstrate the importance of adult literacy to our community; Acceleration to help more adults advance faster; and Public Policy to make state and federal funding for adult literacy more effective.

We know from experience adults can—and do—learn to read. The majority of adults seeking literacy improvement want better jobs. Many others want to contribute to their children's and grandchildren's education. Still others want to learn to read for personal growth, or as one learner described, "I just want to be part of what people do."

For more information on how to become a tutor, build awareness or otherwise support adult literacy, visit www.readingworksdetroit.org.

Paula Brown, CFRE
Executive Director
Reading Works
645 Griswold St., Ste. 2600
Detroit, MI 48226
313-962-6202
www.readingworksdetroit.org

Adult literacy is the gateway issue that impacts the social and economic well-being of metro Detroit. You can help adults gain this essential skill—visit www.readingworksdetroit.org for more information.

NEED MORE COPIES?

Additional copies of the limited, inscribed first edition of *One Cup at a Time,* may be obtained at various sites. Price: $29.95. Inquire about discounts for quantity orders.

Mail or online orders will be filled promptly. Cash, check or money order only, payable to MB Books. No additional charge for Michigan sales tax or shipping & handling.

Locations include:

Brioni Cafe & Deli
7151 N Main St
Village of Clarkston, MI 48346
Phone: (248) 625-6181

Troy Historic Village
60 W Wattles Rd, Troy, MI 48098
Phone: (248) 524-3570

Reading Works
645 Griswold St #2600
Detroit, MI 48226
Phone: (313) 962-6202

MB Books, a unit of MB Communications, LLC
2820 Hummer Lake Road
Ortonville, MI 48462
248 961-3718

By Mail or email:

Reading Works
pbrown@readingworksdetroit.org

MB Books
c/o haneywilliamv@gmail.com

Ebook edition:

Order directly from Amazon for Kindle readers.

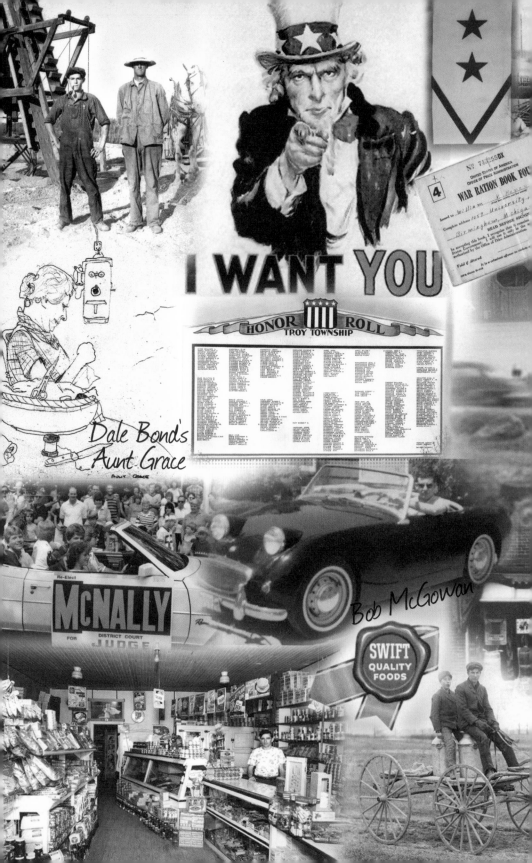

I WANT YOU

HONOR ROLL
TROY TOWNSHIP

Dale Bond's
Aunt Grace

McNALLY
for DISTRICT COURT JUDGE

Bob McGowan

SWIFT
QUALITY
FOODS

WAR RATION BOOK FOUR